M000232632

EVER DATED A PSYCHO?

EVER DATED A PSYCHO?

You don't have to be mad to terrify a loved one...
but it helps!

PAUL DUDDRIDGE

✳ SHORT BOOKS

First published in 2006 by
Short Books
3A Exmouth House
Pine Street, London EC1R OJH

10 9 8 7 6 5 4 3 2 1

A CIP catalogue record for this book
is available from the British Library.

ISBN 10 digit: 1-904977-80-4
13-digit: 978-1-904977-80-3

Printed in Great Britain by
William Clowes Ltd., Beccles, Suffolk

CONTENTS

PART 1

PART 2

PART 3

PART 1

1

WHAT IS A PSYCHO?

It's crucial that before answering the question as to whether you've ever dated a psycho you first understand exactly what a psycho is. Loony, fruitcake, nut, head case, crazed, mad as a March hare and demented, don't begin to cover the unique and distinctive attributes that combine to create these fascinating and beguiling creatures.

Perhaps we should begin with what a psycho is not:

• A psycho is not necessarily insane on the outside – he or she often appears quite sane and sober and reliable, a fully functioning, happy member of society. Indeed, psychos, for the most part, lead perfectly normal lives; they are as capable of holding down a job as they are the partner of whom they are now suspicious.

Psychos are on the increase in all sectors of society. Anthropologists and social historians are split as to the reason why this might be. Some point to a more liberal outlook on all forms of formerly fringe behaviour, a relaxation in social attitudes and a general feeling of live and let live. Others point to the relatively long period that we have gone without a world war. The most likely cause, however, is the phenomenal success of reality TV shows.

Before the advent of the likes of *Survivor*, *Big Brother*, *Beauty and The Geek*, *America's Next Top Model*, *Love Island*, *I'm a Celebrity Get Me Out of Here!* etc., no one would have thought it possible that a living could be earned simply from bed-hopping, bulimia and throwing a tantrum. However, for about six per cent of the population, these are now apparently the passports to a lucrative livelihood.

Where will it all end? In 2004, a British government survey estimated that there were nearly one million psychos – or 'other-headed' people, as they are now charmingly referred to by sociologists – living in the United Kingdom.

The study was prompted by the disturbing number of incidents involving usually normal people sitting outside the home of an ex-partner in a parked car, with only a photo album entitled 'Happy Memories' and a flask of country vegetable soup to keep them company. (NB – the soup turned out to be the variable in this scenario. The hot liquid could just as often turn out to be tea or coffee.)

And that's just your more obvious sort of psycho. It takes all sorts, of course, and this book should prove an indispensable guide to their habits and lifestyles. Read it... and may well never have sex again.

How do you know you have?

You may now be thinking that you have dated a psycho in the past yourself. Well, excuse my scepticism but if you are in any doubt about the matter you probably haven't. The most you may have had is a flirtation with a maniac, a brief encounter with a basket-case or time alone with a loony. The simple rule of thumb is that if you have never doubted yourself and your own behaviour then you have never really dated a psycho.

If you have really dated a psycho, you will have some, if not all, of the following symptoms:

- No friends left
- Deep self doubt

- A fear of the phone ringing
- A preference for staying in
- A deep appreciation of the work of Dr Phil
- A feeling that if you could only try again then you could work it out
- Tinnitus

It's like the thirteenth sign of the zodiac – i.e. whereas an Aries might be given to child-like displays of spontaneity, the psycho will be turning up at your dad's office to quite reasonably point out that you are in cahoots with Satan.

Is psycho behaviour just about jealousy? Goodness, no. Psycho-ness is a complete inability to see the world from any rational point of view, it's about a loss – periodically, and without any warning – of all sense of reality. The middle of the night is an important time in the psycho timetable; it is at this moment that otherwise level-headed partners can turn into whirling, frenzied crazies, either reflecting on something you said that evening or panicking about your imminent behaviour the following day.

Basically, you know you're with a psycho when you can't get away. When a spell banged up alone in a Turkish jail would be a relief.

2

THE PSYCHO FEMALE

It would be easy to dismiss this book as another blatantly misogynist text – were it not for the fact that the best psychos by a mile are women.

The female of the species is uniquely equipped to behave in the cruellest and most bizarre and scary ways imaginable but with the added ability of being able to pass off their anti-social behaviour as some kind of sisterhood feminist protest.

How many of us have laughed uproariously at the stories of men having their suits cut up by their angry wives or jilted girlfriends leaving rotten fish hidden in hard-to-reach places in their ex's bedroom. The sheer horror and aggression of such behaviour is simply shrugged off with a sense of: 'He must have done something to deserve it.'

Well he didn't necessarily do anything to deserve it. There is a double standard at play with the female psycho; she is permitted to act in any way she finds fit without fear of any social admonishment but it is impossible for any man to behave in the same way for fear of him being branded dangerous, unstable or violent. To the female psycho there is always one hard and fast rule – it's always his fault.

Whilst the male psycho might clumsily lash out at the world and any perceived injustices, the female will, if necessary, brood and bubble for an eon, only striking when the revenge that is being served is at its coldest.

I don't want to give the impression that all women are psychos, just the vast majority.

CASE STUDIES

'Joy' to the world!

I like to refer to the young lady in this story as the ironically named 'Joy'.

I met her one New Year's Eve, we hit it off and slept together first thing New Year's Day (so she could keep to her 'not on the first night' rule!). She lived and studied in Cambridge (which was 100 miles from me) so a few weeks later I went to visit her for a couple of days. It went OK and she seemed keen to come and see me. Anyways, long story short, I was out with a friend of mine (female) who was getting a little pissed off because every five or ten minutes my phone would ring and it would be Joy. The frequency of the calls had already pissed me off, which is why I wasn't answering them. At one point I had to answer a call of nature and on my return my friend was wearing a very guilty look. She'd answered my phone and pretended to be my girlfriend with the rather alcohol blurred view that she'd get Joy to stop ringing. Boy was she wrong!

Wondering how I was going to explain that my friend's actions were to stop her incessant phone calls without offending the girl too much, I hit 'busy'. I needed more than three seconds to compose myself. Immediately she rang again; busy. Ring; busy, ring; busy. This began at around 9pm and I'd already had enough after about five minutes and so turned my phone off. Every time I turned it on it rang instantly. At 2am I had to borrow my friends phone to ring a taxi because 'she' was still there on the redial. So far that's five hours straight.

9am the next day I awoke, looked at my phone and turned it on. It rang instantly and it was Joy, still on the redial. Don't know about you, but I'm looking for a far more peaceful start to the day. I'm well and truly pissed off by now so I hit 'busy' like I'm giving her a metaphorical punch and then turned it off again. 11.30am and she's still on the redial. I realised that I was going to have to take action and so took the man's way out and sent her an email explaining what had happened.

I apologised for my friend, explaining that she was a bit drunk and very happily married to another friend of mine called John, and said that I thought her response was a tad scary and please stop ringing me! I turned my phone on and silence, for all of two minutes. Then I start getting texts, emails and phone calls. 11.45am I answered the call, 'Stop ringing me!!! Stop sending texts & stop sending emails.' Scary woman. Thank God she didn't have a car – although she used her head and subscribed me to some dodgy websites, presumably as a substitute for cutting up my clothes and trashing my car.

May I remind you I saw this girl exactly twice, once on New Year and once two weeks later.

She's just a jealous girl

At sixteen I met a girl and we started seeing each other. After only a few weeks she insisted on going down the pub at least an hour before me to make sure there was no one there I could flirt with. I had to get up early, walk to her house and wait for her to get ready before getting a bus to college because she didn't trust me to get on two stops after her. I had to wait for her to collect me after lessons at college and she would tell me who I was and wasn't allowed to talk to. The last straw was her having a go at me because I was on crutches and she couldn't hold my hand and show everyone I was hers.

Wedding Bells

I once had a brief relationship with a young lady who turned out to be absolutely barking (English slang for MAD).

After about two months of going out with her I was bored and fancied one of her not-so-close but a damn-sight-better-looking friends. No contest really, posh but dumpy pug v gorgeous tall thin blonde. Pools panel says, 'Away win'.

So one evening I went round to the pug's flat. I

was half way through the 'I'm-going-to-dump-you'
speech you know, 'it's not you, it's me, I need some
space' when she left the room in tears.

I thought she'd gone to the bathroom for a cry,
but no. She came back into the living room a few
moments later wearing a full length white dress.
'What's that for?' I said.

'It's like the wedding dress I had planned for our
wedding day.'

Eh? 'What wedding day?' We hadn't even dis-
cussed going on holiday, never mind nuptials.

'How can you do this to me? What about the children??' She gasped.

'What children??' I asked incredulously.

'Our children, the ones we were going to have
together, you bastard.'

I did the only thing a true gentleman could have
done in those circumstances – I got my coat and left.

I'm gay!

When my girlfriend and I broke up under pretty bad
circumstances, I assumed we'd never speak again.
She took back her stuff, I took back mine, and we
handed over the spare keys we'd had cut for each

other's flats. What I didn't know was that she'd broken into my email account and spent the best part of a day emailing everyone in my address book a message saying that we'd broken up because I had finally realised that I was gay, that I'd been secretly meeting other gay men in toilets all over London, and that I was happiest when I had another man's cock in my mouth. Bitch.

Marry me?

On our second date we went to dinner with my then girlfriend's parents. Somewhere half-way through the meal, while none of us had had anything to drink (they were teetotal) she started telling them about 'when we get married...' Her parents smiled and nodded and contributed useful hints towards our imminent wedding. Suffice to say there was no imminent wedding, although for some reason I carried on seeing her for a couple of months thereafter, before finally realising it was time to head for the hills.

Down Under

I thought I'd share my tales since I've now recovered

from the psychological wounds.

I had a bad time of it when traveling around Australia as a 21 year old, at the hands of two bunny boilers of the highest order.

The first was a 34-year-old, single youth hostel manager in Adelaide who, after chatting to me whilst I checked in and again when I checked out, somehow became obsessed with me. Having done a round trip around Southern Australia, I checked back in to the youth hostel, and she invited me and the two guys I was traveling with for dinner. At which point she claimed she was in love with me.

I didn't help by shagging her... nor by giving her my mobile number... but from that point on she called, texted and left voicemails obsessively, and suggested she could quit her job and come back to the UK with me. When I say obsessive I mean I was getting about 25 text messages a day... and I sent precisely zero responses. In fact, I'd luckily set up an alternative email account the address of which I gave her. So at least she didn't crash my inbox. Two weeks after I last saw her, she was still trying to call me about five times a day and texting incessantly.

First bunny duly boiled.

I then moved on to Melbourne and signed up

with a recruitment agency. The consultant who inter-
viewed me was mid-thirties and a really good laugh.
A few of my mates temped through her and one day
she invited us to a barbecue she was having. Anyway,
after a few beers, quite a lot of wine, a shrimp or two
and some ' champagne' (i.e. less expensive, less good,
Australian sparkling wine), she suggested we all go to
a club. Once we were there, and even less capable of
telling right from wrong, she swept in for the kill and
again, I was too dumb to say no.

Anyway, she was quite a nice girl, so I saw her a
few times, got a pretty decent pay rise via her agency,
and generally had a good laugh with her. Then I
established she was a divorcee. That wasn't a problem
per se but I realised she was becoming increasingly
needy. For instance, she referred to me on the phone
to one of her friends as her 'boyfriend', which
seemed quite full on after one week and two or three
shags.

Anyway, time came to move on, and she suggested we go for lunch, just the two of us. When I suggested it would be more fun if my mates came too
she started crying and said she couldn't believe I was
still planning on moving on, and that she really wanted me to consider staying, as I was 'special'. This was

less than three weeks after she'd first cornered me in the club. On the last few days before I left Melbourne for Cairns she continually texted me and tried calling. By this stage, I was actually quite worried why I was attracting loons.

Thankfully, once back in Blighty, women of all ages, looks and bunny boiling propensities steered well clear of me as if I were coated in horse shit, and I didn't pull for months. What a relief.

Slapper!

I used to date this absolute psycho who would just flip out for no reason. I dated her for a year and a half and even tried to get out after six months but it was impossible! She would insist that everyone help her choose what to wear and when they didn't I had to help. She would then slap or scratch me then just sit there growling to herself with clenched fists if I didn't choose a proper matching outfit... I was 17 at the time! We would then move on to makeup and contact lenses, which if they hurt her she would take it out on me. She took ages so we were always late for things.

There was one time at Uni when she was getting

ready for a night out and our friends arrived. Not realising she was only in a bra and pants, I walked into the room. She slapped me so hard the mark was instantly visible and purple! She was a complete mad one and I will never be able to forget her for the way she would beat me every so often.

Delete me up before you go go

Last year I started seeing a girl and for the first few weeks everything seemed to be going fine. Then one morning I woke up and checked my mobile for messages. When I looked in the contacts list on my phone all numbers for any females had been deleted. I confronted her about it and she said that in the night she had deleted all numbers off my phone that were stored under a female name. She had even deleted numbers that were family i.e. my mum and my gran! She said I didn' t need any other girls' numbers now I was with her! Psycho! Dumped her on the spot.

Toupee or not toupee?

Last summer I took a job in a student bar in

Leicester. I was one of the only blokes there which was great as I was single. I started having a real laugh with one of the barmaids who I didn't really fancy but got on with all the same. After a few months she asked if I wanted to come out after work and have a drink with her mates. I duly obliged and ended up completely pissed in a taxi with her heading back to my house. After a few cheeky kisses she asked if she could stay and I agreed. When I took my top off she laughed and said I looked like a 10 year old as I didn't have a hairy chest. This was quite embarrassing but we still had a good night. The next weekend the same happened but this time we went back to her house. When we got into her bedroom she laughed once again at my lack of hair. She said not to worry and went into her wardrobe. She came out with a skin-coloured lycra vest covered in artificial hair and asked me to put it on. As I was horny I did but it was extremely itchy. I didn't see her again after that...

Scent of a woman

I went out with a girl who used to love the smell of petrol a little too much. She used to insist we fill the car up ridiculously often and would make me let her hold the petrol cap while I put the petrol in. She would then make me go and pay before putting the cap back on and would sit in the car sniffing it. For her birthday one year, as a joke, I just bought her a jerry can full of petrol – funny thing was she loved it!

Jekyll and Hyde

I dated a girl a few years back who turned into a complete bunny boiler overnight. We'd been with each other for nearly a year with no sign of any trouble at the mill. Then one day she woke up and decided that all of our mutual friends (including my best mate – we had quite a tight group) were bastards and that neither of us should see any of them ever again. She refused to give me any reason for her decision either.

Apart from these 'bastards' we only really had each other. So, eventually I tired of only seeing her all the time and would make excuses to leave her's early and pop over to my mates' houses to see them on the sly. It worked for a while.

One night she became suspicious and called my folks to see where I was (I was still living at home at the time). She found out where I'd been and she phoned me up screaming 'I've smashed a mug over my head because of you!!'? And she had indeed smashed an entire hot mug of tea over her own head when she found out where I was.

I quickly went round to her house to settle things with her, only to find her even more wild. I took her outside to calm her down but this only provoked more madness. She headbutted a tree several times before I could drag her off and then proceeded to start hitting me when I decided to leave.

I eventually managed to flee the fracas and go home somewhat ruffled. I didn't see or hear from her the next day so I popped round to see one of 'the bastards'. I'd only been there a couple of hours when something hit the window... Sure enough she was standing outside in the pissing rain. I asked her to come in from the cold but she screamed back up at me 'Do you know what I've been doing all day?'... no... 'Well I've been smoking crack all day on a train because of you!!'

Needless to say the relationship didn't last much longer than that.

Behind closed doors

Well, there was this one girl... Deleted all the

numbers on my phone, burnt my possessions, put a knife to my throat, beat me up... but what an angel when out with friends and family!

The Rules

I met a girl in a club when I was really drunk and we ended up having a bit of a snog. I took her number and called her a couple of days later to ask her out for a drink. We met up in a bar and it was fine but she was acting a little strange. She was hot and cold with me all evening and I just had no idea where I stood. Then, out of the blue she just went 'I'm not gonna sleep with you you know!' I was a bit taken aback and just said 'err, ok'. She then stood up, said, 'I have to go now' and walked out.

I figured that that was the end of that and didn't think much more of it. Then, about a week later she called demanding to know why I hadn't asked her out again! I politely explained that I had assumed that she wasn't interested due to her behaviour on our date. She burst into tears and started telling me how she was interested and how she'd been trying to follow some dating book on how to get a man and that was why she was acting a bit odd. Hmmmmmm.

She said that she knew that she could be a bit full on and so was trying to play it cool by following the advice in the book. She said she really liked me and could we go out again. I told her that I thought she was a very nice girl but that she wasn't the one for me.

She then proceeded to bombard me with texts and voicemail messages either apologising for being a freak and trying to get me to meet up or shouting and crying about how I was such an insensitive bastard and how she really thought we had a future together. I never returned her calls and she finally gave up and moved on. What a freak!

Smashing break up

I dated a girl at Uni for a while and although I always knew she was a bit nuts, we had fun together. When I did finally end it she wasn't best pleased and, to make it worse, she was living about ten houses down the road at the time. One night, a few weeks after the break up, she saw me leaving my house and came up to talk to me. We had a fairly normal conversation until my mobile rang and I made the mistake of telling her that it was a girl that I was seeing inviting me to meet her and her friends at the pub. My ex snapped when she heard this and started shouting and punching me in the street. I didn't want to cause a scene so I just walked off.

I had a really nice evening with the new girl and managed to convince her to come back to mine. The door was unlocked when we got there but this happened quite a lot so I didn't really think anything of it. I took her up to my room (feeling quite chuffed!) only to find the door had been kicked in and my room trashed – everything completely wrecked! The girl I was with was completely freaked out and I wasn't best pleased either! Only one of my flat mates was in at the time and he told me that my ex had come round in a fit of rage, but that he had been too scared to stop her when he saw the look in her eye. Apparently after she left the house she just stood in the street screaming until someone finally called the police and they came and took her away!

Unsurprisingly, the girl I was with decided that she wanted to go home. I said I'd give her a lift but when we walked to my car we found that my ex had trashed that as well! All the tyres had been slashed, the windows broken and every panel dented. Unfortunately, that was the last time I saw that girl.

Fire fire!

I've been out with a right load of nutters. I was in the house once when it caught on fire. I started to rush out the door and my girlfriend just started putting her make up on in the mirror! I just ran out and left her there and she only came out five minutes later when the fire brigade went in with their hoses!

3

THE PSYCHO MALE

It used to be the case that, like netball and being the Prime Minister of South Korea, being a psycho is only a female pastime. However, in recent years, there has, it seems, been a relaxation of the rules of entry into the world of psychoness, and many men have decided to enter the invigorating world that behaving like a complete fruitcake offers. The latest census reports from around the globe demonstrate that a psycho is now just as likely to be a man as a woman – society may still label sobbing uncontrollably for three days as female behaviour, but it's actually a pursuit being indulged in – quite creatively actually – by an ever-increasing number of males.

The international body that represents the worldwide

interests of the fruit loop community, the Completely Fucking Psycho Organization or the CFPO (not to be confused with the Cornish Fish Producers Organization) estimates that 49.9% of all psychos are men – which represents a year on year increase of 3%. At their last global conference figures showed that by 2012 men will outnumber women in the realm of the oddball.

NB According to its most recent press release the CFPO is due to re-convene whenever it feels like it and when you've stopped judging it and staring at it.

CASE STUDIES

Rupert the Bear

I once dated a bloke called Rupert – well that's what he called himself because he had an obsession with Rupert the Bear. He would always wear check trousers, braces and wanted to go down the woods all the time, even at night. He said he liked looking at the trees because it made him feel good. The trouble was, when he arrived home, he'd demand that I took his check trousers off and give him a good spanking for 'being late home' until his bum was red raw. He would then put on his teddy bear pyjamas and just eat bananas. I tried to tell him that only monkeys eat bananas, if he wanted to pretend to be an animal, but he never took any notice. What a freak.

Night caller

This guy used to hide in a neighbour's garden to watch me and my house in the small wee hours. To avoid leaving footprints he used to remove his shoes. Unbeknownst to him the neighbours invested in a new security system including high beam lights and direct dial to the police. As the garden lit up like Blackpool illuminations he legged it, shoes in hand, and hid for over an hour in a nearby churchyard while the police, who weren't very busy that night, kept circling the area. We even found out later that the garden he hid in was the owned by the IT guy who consulted on his business!

He was banned from driving any of the company vehicles at night in his family's attempts to curtail his night-time activities. Undeterred, he nicked a van to drive to my house. He was so worked up he missed his turn off and reversed up a slip road so hard that he knocked over a lamp post, caved in the back of the van and wrote it off. He continued on to my house and returned the van in the morning. His family said I was partly responsible as he had been thinking about me when it had happened. I was nineteen at the time and he was 34.

One night he persuaded me back to his flat. He left at 10am to get us some breakfast. By 1pm I was worried and tried to leave. He had locked all the doors and taken the keys with him. By 4pm I climbed out of the six foot high lounge window, scaled the six foot (locked) back gate and was legging it to the bus stop. He saw me getting on the bus and started screaming like a banshee running alongside as the bus pulled away. When the bus pulled up at the lights he hammered on the doors to be let on. Some chance! When this proved ineffective he hurled his shopping at the doors – including six eggs, bacon and a string of sausages!

Another time, he brought a lesbian of our acquaintance round and told her she could have two hours with me, while he sat on the garden wall out-side. Needless to say I declined this 'generous'offer. She, on the other hand, was quite persistent!

RSPCA

My ex was absolutely gorgeous but a bit of a nut job. He once punched his hand through a glass window when I wouldn't give him my last ten quid to bet on the horses and once wrecked my mate's car because I was talking to her and not him. I had a budgie (don't ask, it was a rescued one) and even though I had finished with this guy, he was still in the flat. I was at work and he called telling me to get home and if I didn't he would kill my budgie. I didn't believe him as he was always making stupid threats but I got home and he had broken its neck! I had to move 250 miles away to get away from him. When he did find me he got his mum to call me crying and begging me to just talk to him. I didn't and eventually he moved away and I was able to move back to my town.

Fiji wedding

I dated a complete weirdo who was my manager at my part time Uni job. I thought he was quite cute but after a week he loved me, after two weeks he wanted to go on holiday and after three weeks he wanted it to be a honeymoon/wedding abroad!

When we went out he started telling people we

were engaged and that we were having a baby and were getting married in Fiji. He got all these brochures and all that for it – I was well scared. I dumped him after six weeks and only stayed with him that long cos he was my manager and I was too scared to dump him. He then found out where I lived back home in Manchester, followed me home, followed me to work even after HE got fired and stood outside for an hour and 45 minutes!

He was soooo weird! And then he harassed me with messages and calls for about eight weeks after. He's stopped now but I found out that he had done it to a girl before me in Preston.

He well scared me!

Juggernaut

Yep, first date at some place I'd never been before, my psycho takes me for a walk in the darkness and decides to tell me all about the time he got run over by a juggernaut (he had his back to it apparently) and how he loves to remember the feeling of waking up in hospital with all the bones sticking up out of his legs.

He showed me a great network of scars in order

to impress me and then made ME walk HIM to his bus stop 'cause we were in a rough part of town!

Mr Not-So Perfect

I went out with a lovely bloke, well I say went out, but we didn't actually go out together because he wouldn't be seen in public with me. I really should've heard the alarm bells from the off.

But you know how you think it will improve, 'he likes me really' you tell yourself, 'I mean otherwise, why does he want to see me every night?' And he did. He told me he hated being in his own home when I wasn't there – ahhh, sweet, I felt myself really falling for him.

And that was the problem. I was genuinely as hooked as I thought he was. So I waited, and waited, and waited, until eventually he said he would take me out to dinner.

Oh what joy, I was so excited! I got dressed up and turned up at his house only to see him chewing. 'Hang on a minute, what's that I smell? Food?'

'You've eaten? But what about our dinner?'

'We'll go anyway' he says. He obviously thinks this is a big treat for me. So we turn up at the restaurant, and I order to eat alone whilst he sits opposite me playing with his Blackberry.

We don't talk much as I'm eating and he's pretty busy online. Then we get back home in time to see what he had on Sky Plus for later.

Well stupidly at the time I was so besotted with him that I didn't care what we did, I just wanted to be with him. The relationship wasn't perfect but I was convinced he was. I didn't even mind being a secret at first but after six months it got a bit insulting.

I was often told that he would tell people about me, but it never happened, and despite all his declarations of how fabulous his life was with me in it, and he couldn't live without me, I just got a call one day, out of the blue, saying 'Oh, I don't know, I think we should just knock this on the head.'

The next time I saw him was a few weeks later with a girl on his arm and he just walked straight passed me in the street and ignored me. They were both dressed up heading to Soho, so I would imagine she was being taken out.

Oh, and the next time I saw him he was having dinner with another girl, and then another, as so it goes on.

Battery operated

I once went out with a guy who after just one dinner date and a drink in the local pub began to 'worry' about the fact that I was working nights with other men who could do very bad things to me (lucky me eh?) Anyway, he took it upon himself to sit outside my office from 6am every morning and when I went down to ask him what he thought he was playing at he said that he was 'buying batteries' (WHATEV-ER!) He then rang my house every day, every half hour until I actually had to change my telephone number. He then tried to sneak back into my life by trying to buy a washing machine from my brother!

Scrubber

I met this guy in a bar and we ended up dating for six months. I only found out after we broke up that whenever we had a big argument he would use my toothbrush to clean the soles of his feet!

Suicidal

I dated a guy who threw himself down the stairs and then tried to convince our friends that I'd pushed him. The only problem was that I'd been sat in the lounge with them the whole time.

On another occasion, the same guy passed out from an alcohol overdose. I walked him round for four hours and fed him coffee as he refused to go to the hospital. At one point he said he needed to pee, and went into the bathroom, then passed out and cracked his nose on the bath. All the thanks I got was him telling people I'd punched him in the face.

When I finally dumped him, in an attempt to get back with me he invited me for a drink with his best friend from London who I had never met. After sitting in the pub for four hours with the two of them he then starts accusing me of having an affair with his mate. His mate had moved to London when I was 14 and had not been home since!!!!!

Cutting remarks

I had one boyfriend who cut his hands with a scalpel because I came home from the pub half an hour late. There was one who used to cry if I told him he was putting on weight and another one who fought everything in sight and cleaned his teeth with a penknife.

Cling-on

I went out with the biggest psycho going and he still won't leave me alone to this day! We went out last year for eight and a half months when I was 17 and he was 18. I tried to end it in the October as I didn't have any feelings for him anymore but unfortunately he wouldn't accept that.

He went mad threatening to kill himself and crying down the phone a lot for the first few days. Then, the funniest moment was when I was lying in bed one night and he got a stepladder up to my bedroom trying to get into my house! What a loser! It was all because I refused to talk to him – as if that was going to work! At the time I was scared to death and rang everyone and anyone to come and save me out of the house – now I manage to look back and laugh. Still, three months later he calls me at all hours and all the time, chatting pure rubbish to try and get me back. The kid's a psycho and won't ever let go I don't think.

Hedging his bets

Ha, don't get me started! What about the ex who accused me of being unfaithful because the top of my toothpaste tube was hard! Or the one who accused me of saying he had a small willy because we were talking about garden hedges and I said I preferred the smaller ones!

Stayin' Alive

One time I met a tall dashing chap at a Beegees tribute concert (I just stumbled in there, I had no idea, honest!) I soon realised that he actually thought they were the Beegees and proceeded to get all the tribute bands' autographs!

I ended up going back to his place where he led me into his paisley, doiley-tastic living room complete with drawings and picture upon picture upon endless picture of the late Diana princess of Wales! Beginning to feel a little freaked out (OK I was naive) he asked me if I would like him to play a song for me. Before I could answer, he whipped out the old Casio, set it to demo and proceeded to 'play' (there was very little finger movement, more just the demo) whilst singing very badly. He then played me a CD of his that he had recorded – a cheap cheesy production deal with him singing Boyzone or something equally bad.

Suffice to say I nodded through with a tortured smile on my face as I balanced on the edge of the grannytastic two-seater sofa. Sad as it sounds I did actually go to bed with him but then had a moment of realisation and ran away while he was still in the bathroom! Nightmare but funny.

4
THE PSYCHO COUPLE

Researchers in the exciting world of psycho dating describe the psycho couple as a relatively rare occurrence. This is not because psycho couples are uncommon. It's just that such couples cannot usually stay together for very long before they either burn out or attempt to kill each other.

The very state of being a psycho (even one of the cripplingly shy sort) is one which needs an audience. How can any self-respecting psycho gain full recognition for their magnificently mad plumage if their partner is busy shouting at a complete stranger in a bar for having the audacity to ask if that chair is free?

The natural home of any psycho couple is, of course, the counsellor's office. This is the arena where both parties feel most alive. It is the ley line of the psycho couple, the one place on earth where their uniqueness can be welcomed, appreciated and if necessary scored out of ten.

Indeed you will probably be interested to know that couples counselling was first developed to observe psycho couples at close range. It was only some years down the line that, due to the brevity of the psycho couple relationship, counsellors found themselves forced to move on to more lucrative and sustainable client bases – hence their evolving interest in normal couples. i.e two people who have a problem communicating and want to salvage their long-term partnership. (Such are the demands of business, even in the sensitive world of relationship therapy: of course, any counsellor worth his or her salt will tell you that they would much prefer to be faced with the excitement of two absolute fucking nut jobs trying to kill each other than deal with a rather mundane discussion about the pain and shame of erectile dysfunction.)

CASE STUDIES

Call my bluff
I went out with a bonkers bird for seven years.

One night I woke up not being able to breathe. I quickly realised that the nutter was choking me in her sleep and nearly had to break her wrists to make her stop!

She went really psycho in the end, proper like 'Don't go out, don't leave me, I'll kill myself, I'll slit my wrists, take pills!' blah blah blah. She freaked me right out for about six months until I sat her down and called her bluff. Only way to beat a nutter is to 'outnut' them!

Perfectly sane now though me. Honest.

Keep left

My mate has this weird thing where she has to walk on the left-hand side of people. It's slightly bizarre and really quite annoying! She says it just feels really really wrong to be on the other side. The thing is, she met this guy who seemed pretty cool, but it turned out he has the same issue! Walking down the street with them was just a complete nightmare because they would both spend the whole time battling to walk on the left! They only lasted about five months before it all became too much and they split up. They are still friends though and I always make sure I politely decline any invitations that involve actually walking anywhere...

His mother's hall of fame

I dated a psycho and his even more psycho mother! They had an incestuous relationship where she would kiss him on the lips all the time and she even had a wall of fame in her hallway of all the ex-girlfriends she managed to split her son up from! He had an extremely bad temper, smashed his fist through an airplane TV screen, threw a bottle at a co-worker, slept with my friends under my nose while I was sleeping in the next room... need I go on?!!

Sofa so good

They say true love is blind but this relationship was a real eye opener!

Here are a few examples:

• When my girlfriend moved in to my flat I had to sleep on the sofa bed because I fidgeted in bed.

• The night my grandmother died I had to take my girlfriend out and cheer her up because she was depressed about her job.

• I was told to buy flowers every two weeks, but when I got them they ended up in the bin because she didn't like them.

• She would wait outside the toilet asking about the noises I was making and why I was spending so long on the toilet.

• To finish off, when we split up, I was told that I'd be lucky to find another girl like her. I am very glad I've never been that lucky again.

Sweet revenge

I think I may be the psycho in this story but it felt justified at the time! I worked at a posh hotel in New York and hooked up with a stupidly rich city boy hot shot who was staying there. He said all the right things and I believed him until I found out that he'd been playing me all along, in a most public manner. During this time he had moved hotels to make things easier for me as I wasn't supposed to fraternise with the clients.

So, I went round to where he was staying and gave him (and me!) one last shag and then stayed the night. He went out the next day and I stayed and absolutely trashed the room! I pretty much totalled the place, cut all of his clothes up and ordered all of the most expensive things I could find on the menu. There were no accurate reports of the total bill, but I estimated it to be in the tens of thousands of dollars! I think he learnt his lesson.

5

LIVING WITH YOUR PSYCHO

The pure-bred psycho will waste no time at all in moving in with you (it will always be him or her who moves in with you), as they have no accommodation of their own and are given to wandering the earth between relationships. Most eastern European legends pertaining to vampires and were-wolves, by the way, have been shown by folklore historians to be thinly veiled metaphors for the activities of the psycho.

Once your psycho has parked him or herself in your life and home, do not even think of trying to come to some sort of parity vis a vis domestic chores or budget management.

The psycho partner is incapable of taking on any more

than their already above average (emotional) task load, so an equal distribution of chores is most unlikely ever to take place. Your psycho will be far too busy watching daytime TV or inviting an ever-expanding group of unsuitables back to the love-nest for a drink to ever find the opportunity to flick a duster round or put out the bins.

NB In the case of OCD-suffering cleanliness fanatics, the advantages of their strenuous efforts to hoover both above the carpets and beneath, and generally re-fold all the sheets in the linen cupboard 5,000 times are soon completely outweighed by the furious rows that erupt daily, during which destruction and havoc will be wreaked throughout the house.

CASE STUDIES

Completely arm-less

I once went out with a guy who had to have his arm around me wherever we went. My head was permanently fixed in his armpit and the only time he didn't have his arm around me in public was when I was driving, hence I drove EVERYWHERE! When I asked him why he was like that ALL the time he said that he found it comforting!? FREAK!

Just the two of us

After going out with my ex girlfriend for almost a year we decided that it would be a good time to move in together. I thought she was great and truly loved her until we started living together. She, almost overnight, turned into this obsessive mother figure who started treating me like her five-year-old son. This could be ok in that all my meals were cooked for me and clothes washed. But on the flip side it was hideous! I was told that I HAD to be home by seven at the latest and always had to take her packed lunch into work. If I was going out I had to tell her exactly where, when, with who and for how long. If I couldn't provide these answers she would come with me. She started buying all my clothes (Marks and Spencer) and reading me bedtime stories. It was my dad who persuaded me to leave, which I did but only after a few 'mother/son' arguments!

Check up

Dated and married a psycho! When we were dating

he would follow me, record me when he went out, check my phone, e-mails etc. He was very possessive but I didn't really care about him checking on me cos I loved him and there wasn't anything to find. I thought it would get better once we were married but he continued using dating agencies, checking on me and harassing his ex! It all got a bit much in the end so I got out. Definitely learnt a lesson in trust from that one!

From a Russian with love

Had the amazing misfortune that after several years with a total possessive nutcase I escaped, married a lovely Russian girl I met on holiday, until she ended up pulling every single plant out of my garden and pushing them through my letterbox!

Bigger and better

I went out with a guy when I was younger who I thought was lovely. That was until he started calling my mum, 'mum'! He was really possessive and even joined my drama group so that he could keep an eye on me. He slept in his car and followed me. When I finished with him he would stalk me at work, turn up at work with presents, and basically follow me every-where I went. He phoned me and told me he knew my parents were away and that he knew how to get into my house! In the end I got a new boyfriend – a very big boyfriend who frightened him off!

Up the duff

I went out with a girl for about three years. I was completely in love with her and everything was great. When she told me she was pregnant I was a bit shocked and completely shitting myself but we decid-ed that it was what we wanted and that we would try and make it work. I took a second job to try and save up some extra cash and generally tried to come to terms with the fact that my life was going to change for ever.

A few months down the line something just didn't feel right. She wasn't putting on any weight and wouldn't let me come to the doctor or any of her other appointments with her. It all came to a head one night when I confronted her and, after the initial 'HOW DARE YOU ACCUSE ME OF LYING YOU INSENSITIVE BASTARD!!!' she completely broke down. She told me that she'd lied because she thought I was going to leave her and that it was the only way I'd stay with her. I packed my bags there and then and walked out. A few months later I bumped into one of her mates and found out that she was seeing someone new and was actually pregnant with his child! I' m so glad I got out when I did!

Hygiene freak

I briefly went out with a guy who was a bit of a clean freak. He was always immaculately dressed and the kind of guy who would never even dream of wearing the same pants two days in a row. He ironed his socks and made everyone put on slippers when they came to his house. The weirdest thing though was that he used to spend at least 20 minutes in the bathroom after sex. I thought this was a bit odd as in my experience men don't usually even manage to stay awake that long afterwards(!) but I didn't quite have the guts to ask what the hell he was doing in there. When I did finally confront him about it, it turned out that he had serious issues about contact with other people and the germs he might pick up. He would therefore go into the bathroom and wash his entire body with Dettol to try and disinfect himself! Looking back, you'd think the smell would've given it away really but I guess I was the one who couldn't stay awake.

Bill Oddy

My last boyfriend is mad! He used to make animal noises in bed, like a fox, shaking and snuffling for food. He would even claw the bed at night and run in bed on the spot... why? Plus he was a habitual liar, making up massive lies like the fact he was going to inherit fifteen million quid, yet I know he was signing on and living in a council flat. All very worrying as he 40 years old. He's living in his own 'universe'.

Marriage Hell

Dated? I went on to marry him thinking 'Hmmm, I'll take care of that!' He and I were paramedics so we worked odd and long hours. If I didn't answer my phone when he thought I should be in, he'd have a rampage on my answering machine.

One night I was too tired to bother checking my machine and I was in bed when there was a pounding on the door. I went to the door and it was 'him'.

'I know you have someone in there – let me in!'

So, I let him in. He whizzed through my flat checking the closets and the shower and (surprise surprise) found no one. He then proceeded to check my answering machine and yes, there was a message. It was from a bloke who had returned to school and had asked me to help tutor him in physics and chemistry.

Well the guy I was dating knew the other guy and went ballistic and beat to death my answering machine! He then followed it up by throwing nick-nacks at anything to hand around my flat before pulling my fuses and leaving me in the dark!

It was a stormy thirteen years of on-again off-again dating and a number of engagements (like ten or twelve) before he actually set a date to get married (while drunk at a barbeque.) I thought 'if I marry him these jealous rages will come to an end'.

Was I ever wrong – he was worse! Controlling who I had as friends, what I wore, when and where I worked etc. In the end I realised it wasn't worth it and got as far away as possible.

Smashing TV

A girlfriend once threw a TV at me during an argument. It was a big old one in a heavy chipboard case – I could barely lift it and I used to work on a furniture truck and she's a svelte 50 kilo Asian gal so it amazed me that she could actually pick it up and then hurl it across the room at me! Afterwards I put it back, plugged it in, turned it on and it worked better than ever! They don't make 'em like that anymore.

She also came at me with a knife and routinely smashed glass objects d'art in jealous rages over imagined infidelities. It turned out that it was her that was carrying on multiple affairs behind my back so I guess it was guilt not jealousy after all – weird huh?

Work 'mate'

I was 'casually seeing' this guy from work. I didn't know him very well as he had only just started working for us a couple of months earlier and generally kept himself to himself. I just thought he was shy. Actually he was just fucking mad. To give you an overall impression of this guy, he was 6' 7" tall, fairly stocky and ginger. He went to work in our other office for a while, and when he returned, he decided to take the empty seat behind me – we work in an open-plan Architects office. Here is a typical example of the day I would experience:

I arrive at work. He arrives 30-45 mins late. He sits down and says my name over and over until I stop what I'm doing and look around – this is usually about five times. He then asks if I'd like a cup of tea. I say no thanks, as I already have one. 20 mins later he repeats the tea chant. I say no thanks. This will be repeated at 20 minute intervals throughout the day. Eventually he will get incredibly stroppy and ask why his tea isn't good enough for me. He is deadly serious. He literally throws his rattle out of the pram if I make myself one and don't ask him if he'd like a drink.

I am suddenly aware that there is someone behind me. He's standing behind me staring at whatever I'm doing, so close that I can feel his breath. He just stands there looking at me, saying nothing, just staring. I'm then aware that he is going through my bag, and I mean properly rummaging through my bag. I turn around to see what he's doing and he just looks at me, smiles and walks away. I am speechless. He also goes through my post, and will tell me what is in my pigeon hole before I look.

He will, at least 20 times a day, jump up, flap his arms and shout 'I hate working here. I'm wasting my life', 'this is fucking useless, a complete waste of my time' or simply 'fucking bollocks'? I sit next to two senior associates. They hear this too. He will suddenly, and at the top of his tone deaf voice start singing or whistling. He will also do this when standing staring over my shoulder.

He will ask me questions all day, using the tea chant method to get my attention. These questions include such classics as: 'What do Apricots taste like?' 'My Risotto isn't fat, what am I doing wrong?' 'Is it normal to drink a bottle of wine every day?' 'Where do I get extra long jeans from?'

Oh, and he is addicted to internet dating sites and spends all of his remaining day on the phone making personal calls.

I caught *What Women Want* on TV the other night. There's a scene were a woman is looking at the irritating wanker thinking 'I wish you'd never seen me naked'... Welcome to my world. Needless to say, we are not casually seeing one another anymore.

Green with envy

After joining a new job in the city I found myself in the position of a possible promotion. The boss had said that I was the perfect candidate and put me forward. Lo and behold I got it. I was extremely excited and rushed home to tell my girlfriend. Instead of being happy she said that I was patronising her by taking the job and that I shouldn't accept it. I convinced her that it was best for both of us and she eventually agreed. A month later I was awarded employee of the month for my work and given a holiday for two at a health spa. On giving my girlfriend the news she burst into tears, calling me chauvinistic, arrogant and selfish and ran up to our room. It wasn't long before I left her altogether.

6

SPLITTING UP WITH A PSYCHO

Breaking up is ridiculously hard to do. To the point of dangerous.

If you have decided that the realm of the psycho is perhaps just a little too taxing for you, if you find yourself severely lacking in the tolerating-sitting-in-casualty-3-nights-running department then let me first extend my deepest sympathies to you. You have obviously enjoyed the highs and lows of the greatest relationship fun you will ever know. For you all that is left is the nostalgia of accounting for your movements between leaving work and coming home. Being telephoned thirty times a day from a private number will fade fondly into the past as you try forlornly to rebuild your life armed only with a partnership based on sanity, trust and understanding.

First, though, you must do the deed. You must LEAVE your psycho.

This is easily said, it is easily written about; but of course it is one of the hardest of all achievements. Indeed, many have ended up simply marrying the oddball in question in order to avoid the uncomfortable and potentially life-threatening confrontation that invariably ensues.

It is estimated that up to 30 per cent of identity thefts are carried out by partners who are too terrified to ditch a psycho face to face, and plan to start a new life under an assumed name.

CASE STUDIES

I'll be waiting

I recently made the huge mistake of starting a 'thing' with an old friend. I kissed him one day and he stayed for about five. He used to go in for the kiss with his eyes half shut – ugh, it still grosses me out now! So after about two weeks I started getting 'The Headache' and after about four weeks I decided that enough was enough and so tried to end it. His response was that we would end up together, but that he was happy to give me space.

Fast forward four months to when I was out at a friend's birthday. I was blissfully unaware that he was stalking me on the dance floor until I kissed this other guy and he comes barging over, reefs me off him and demands to know what I was doing – duh! So, after managing to get rid of him without too much of a scene I went back to the new guy. So me and this new guy decided to go to another club and were getting into the cab when psycho guy pulled me out of the cab and started dragging me off with him, crying 'Don't do this to me please!' His friend jumped in, broke him away from me, threw me back in the cab, and dragged psycho away. He ended up sending the obligatory 'you're fucked' text messages to me all night and then came to see me the next day like nothing had happened! He asked me out for drinks that night and I ended up having to tell him that I was seeing the new guy again.

So since then he's decided that although I'm still in love with him, I'm in denial, but he will always be waiting (he told my flatmate that). But he's decided that he can't see me in the meantime as it hurts too much but when I'm ready, he'll be there. Hello?

Delusional? I went out with him for four weeks, four months ago! Oh and he also threw a hamburger at me once when he thought I was trying to pick up someone, which I wasn't – I was just talking to another friend.

Get over it!

My ex-boyfriend had clearly never got over his wife leaving him. Even after we'd been together for a few months his house was still in the half-decorated state it was in when she had walked out. He kept their unopened wedding presents in the cupboard (yes the marriage was that brief) and when I also gave him the elbow he 'borrowed' customers' cars from work so he could sit outside my flat every night and not be identified.

Another ex tipped paint stripper over my car completely writing it off, and subscribed me to a magazine that had the same name as the club we met in. He also hacked into my email account, read my emails and then pretended one of my group of friends was passing information to him, leaving me a bit of a paranoid wreck.

When me and my new bloke (very normal and

nice) went away for Valentine's Day, the ex did some detective work, got the name of the hotel, phoned ahead and cancelled!

Give up gracefully I say!

Water Closet

My ex-boyfriend hid overnight in a storage cupboard outside my flat front door and when I opened the door to leave for work he rushed into the flat, into the bedroom flung open the wardrobe and stole my underwear. I later found that he had pooed in the outside cupboard. On another occasion, he returned a tee-shirt that I'd given him for his birthday (left it on the 'welcome' mat outside the front door) and promptly weed on it. See a theme coming through here?

Towel for one

I once slept with a girl after a party. In the morning I made it quite clear that it had just been a drunken thing and I didn't want to see this girl anymore. She took it surprisingly well, gave me a towel, and suggested I have a shower to freshen up before I left.

While I was showering, she cut off the front half of my shoes with a breadknife, scissored up my bank cards, and poured a whole bottle of vinegar over my suit, shirt, and pants. She also called her brother, who lived just down the road, and was there waiting when I came out of the bathroom. He was an amateur boxer. I had to walk home in nothing but a wet towel, with all my stuff in a Sainsbury' s carrier bag.

Trouble brewing

I went out with this one girl who wouldn't let me out of the flat unless I had a university lecture. I had to come back and prove to her I had been there and only there. I never cheated on her to make her think I wouldn't be trusted. Whenever I returned she was crying in my bed, thinking I'd been with someone else. She had a picture of me blown up and made into a cardboard cut out, which she took shopping with her, but left in the car (with the windows open for air!) She also once pulled her eye lashes out and sent me them on Valentine's Day in an envelope. In the note it said she wanted me to brew them up and drink the juice, no sugar.

I'm slightly worried as I finally ended it six

months ago and she's still telling everyone we're an item. I am now seriously contemplating leaving the country.

Paint job

My first 'proper' boyfriend when I was sixteen years old was a complete and utter ginger psychopath (him Scorpio, me Aquarius – not a good mix).

After four months of going out he started commenting on my revealing clothes and the friends I kept. I was a proper northern chav bird then, not the suave media blonde that I am now! After six months I was sick of the whole thing and decided to dump him. That night, after the deed had been done, he came to my dad's house, shouted at me and chucked yellow paint over my dad's car, which he found close to hand in the drive when shouting. He then proceeded to beat up my dad and attempt to beat up my 6' 2" brother. This continued on until I called the cops and got him arrested.

The next day my mum made me take a court injunction out against him, but three days later I was sneaking back to be with him – crazy chick that I was, sixteen, and obviously attracted to the 'danger factor'. One week later we're in a nightclub with friends and I'm talking to this boy and the crazy ginger nutter suddenly gets jealous, shouts, screams and the next thing I know I'm dripping with blood and I've got a bottle stuck in my head! Not nice when you're wearing your mate's white skirt!!!

It certainly taught me a very good lesson in love at a very early age.

Heart break

I went out with this boy when we were at school. His name was Steve and he was a drummer in a death metal band called 'Rellik' (it's killer backwards – I should've known then!) and their big crowd pleaser was 'Dead puppy'. Man I thought he was cool....for a while.

He was heartbroken at the tender age of 16 when I dumped him. My mum and I went to a play at the local school and when we came out we found a shoebox in her car. Inside the shoebox he had put dead roses and the champagne flute from our leaver's disco (smashed of course) and had written on the lid of the box 'help me I'm inside'.

A few weeks later...

I worked at a toy shop in the local shopping centre and one Halloween the kids were 'trick or treating' around all the shops. I saw this one guy lurking about, walking very slowly back and forth dressed in black and wearing a Jason mask. I thought he was creepy but not in a bad way – I mean it was Halloween! Later I saw his friends and they asked if I'd seen Steve that night...guess what costume he was wearing! When I came out of work the tyres were flat on my little Ford escort and he had smashed the bonnet leaving footprints all over it. I had a friend at the police station who went round to his house to scare him. He made him get his trainers and told him he was going to match them up to my car and that he would go to jail! I didn't have much trouble with him after that.

Obsessive Compulsive 3 times

I once dated a woman for a couple of months who at first appeared completely level-headed. For a while all was well, and then I realised all was not well, when her Obsessive Compulsive Disorder came to light.

This woman wasn't crippled by her condition like some unfortunates. In fact upon reflection a compulsive gas stove or light switch checker would have meant my flat would always be in safe hands! This woman had to do everything three times, from the inconsequential to the important. For example, sex: she had to orgasm three times before midnight if the act was started before then. (I'm just glad I never started at ten to twelve!)

If something wasn't done in a three she felt the world was going to end. With regards to dressing, she had to take her clothes off and put them on three times before she would get in bed. I never realised this for the first month or so as I thought she was being romantic, ('I'll get ready, and you meet me in five minutes' kind of thing).

As I realised what was happening, the little things started to get me; saying goodbye three times is acceptable and even normal sounding if punctuated randomly. But saying hello three times on the trot made her sound like a policeman! If I said goodbye twice, she would even phone me back for me to say it that one more time.

Buying apples, changing TV channels, dividing food into portions (now that was annoying as there were generally only two of us eating), turning lights on and off, and even pouring sugar into Coffee – I only take one bloody spoonful.

My mates were of no use, laughing at my pain! How do you dump a girl with an increased sexual appetite? Surely it's perfect? I did not agree,

When I concluded the relationship, I kid you not, she made me say it three times, and then she was OK.

Bizarre…

7

THE UPSIDES

This book may have given the impression that having a psycho in your life is a problem and that their behaviour causes nothing but trouble. This is far from the case, in fact more and more people have realised the benefits of partnering a psycho and are exploiting the many advantages that a wacko can bring to their life:

- There is always someone home to sign for deliveries
- The house is always clean
- Even the most badly behaved neighbours don't bother you
- The running away keeps you fit

- You have enough pharmaceutical knowledge to retrain as a chemist
- You were never going to get someone that attractively packaged unless the contents were a bit dented
- You have convenient access to the complete works of Dr Phil
- You'll have plenty of stories to tell your grandchildren

This last point perhaps needs a bit of expansion, as it really is one of the greatest things to be said for having a psycho partner.

We all enjoy taking photographs at important stages in our lives. We treasure the memories that photographs rekindle. The simple act of opening a photo album can remind us of a happy, romantic or important event. In fact, scientists now claim that smell is the most powerful of all the senses for triggering memory. Maybe the smell of an exercise book reminds you of your first day of school, or the inimitable aroma of a good Sunday roast can bring all those joyous family lunches flooding back.

Well, this is all very well; but there is always the chance of losing a camera, inadvertently destroying the film and therefore your sweet memories. You may suffer from hay fever or a simple cold that can prevent you soaking up the subtle aromatic nuances that will in the future help you recall that romantic walk. And that's to say nothing of the most probable memory hazard: just too much going on your life to leave enough room in your head to remember anything at all.

So it is crucial that you take every necessary step to ensure other ways of protecting your personal history. And the safest and most obvious way to do this is, of course, to make sure that either you, or a member of your family, or at least one of your close friends is dating a psycho.

That heavenly walk barefoot in the sand on that exotic beach is far less likely to make it into the memory banks without the aide-memoir of your psycho lover storming off and shouting obscenities at you and all the other couples on the shore-line.

Watch out for these important days/events in the psycho calendar. They rarely pass without unfortunate incident and so will be stored in your memory-bank for ever:

- Christmas
- Other people's weddings
- Any family event
- Holidays

- Valentine's Day
- Friends' dinner parties

CASE STUDIES

Here comes the bride

I went to the wedding of a friend of mine with my boyfriend at the time. We hadn't been going out that long but as far as I knew it was going well. He got on really well with my mates, which is very important to me, and I was starting to think it could be going somewhere.

There were lots of people at the wedding who I hadn't seen in ages so I ended up spending a lot of time away from my boyfriend. He was happy enough just drinking (a lot it turns out!) and chatting with my mates so I didn't worry about it too much. A very good male friend of mine asked me to dance and I honestly didn't think anything of it. Until that was, my boyfriend came drunkenly barging on to the dance floor, pulls him away from me and punches him in the face! I was gob smacked and just stood there not quite knowing how to react – that was until he burst into tears! All he kept saying was that he was so sorry and he never meant it to happen like this! He then proceeded to declare his undying love for the friend that I'd been dancing with! I was literally speechless! My friend also looked a bit surprised to say the least and politely forgave him for punching him in the mouth and explained that although he liked him as a friend, he wasn't that way inclined!

I ended up comforting the (now ex!) boyfriend for the next hour or so and then putting him in a cab home. Luckily when we spoke the next day we both managed to see the funny side and just ended up laughing about it for about half an hour!

Naked

I once went on a blind date with a very wealthy stockbroker who took me to the Ivy. We had a very enjoyable evening and he offered to drive me home. Being the polite girl that I am, I invited him in for a coffee (totally meaning a coffee!) and stood in the kitchen, filled the kettle, asked him if he wanted coffee or tea, got out all the cups etc. Then I asked him to excuse me whilst I went to the loo and having taken off my coat, went into the bathroom.

I can't have been more than one minute but when I came out he was standing butt naked in my lounge with a huge stiffy. I said 'You're naked' and he said 'I have an erection' – like I was going to throw a party or something – and I said 'But you're naked!' and he said 'but I have an erection'.

It was then that I noticed that he had even managed to fold his clothes up perfectly and put them on the sofa – how he managed that in such a short amount of time I don't know!

I wasn't sure if he thought I would be turned on by his nakedness or maybe he had seen it in a film or something but it took quite a lot of discussion about how 'a cup of coffee' doesn't mean 'have a blow job' before I could convince him to put his clothes on and get out of my house!

There were no more dates to The Ivy or anywhere else for that matter!

PART 2

8

THE PSYCHO AND FOOD

Food plays an enormous role in the life of the psycho. Indeed, all psychos are always on some kind of eating regime.

Western diets have been altered considerably in the last fifty years due partly to nutritionists enlightening us all about the dangers of over indulgence in fats, sugars and processed food and partly to nut jobs refusing to eat what's in front of them – making the rest of us traipse round some health food shop looking for palm oil to help make some vile concoction that assists detoxification.

This has been of huge assistance to the psycho, for whom fad diets and health food are bread and chips. Think about it. No matter how bad tempered or volatile a qualified chef might appear, not a single one in the history of mankind has been a psycho.

On the other hand, all picky eaters, over-eaters, gluten-allergists, no-wheat-no-dairy fanatics, macro-psychotics, blonde bingers, red-meat haters and non-religious vegetarians are undoubtedly psychos. (NB To some extent a non-religious veggie diet should be encouraged because it can weaken the psycho sufficiently to render their blows painless and to make them slow enough to enable you to run away.)

However, although eating disorders are deeply associated with psycho behaviour, do be careful not to oversimplify one of this most fascinating and complex features of the psycho.

Because there *are* psychos who do love to eat and they like food and they love to go to restaurants. At least they like to plan to go to restaurants. To really enjoy the full range of the psycho on the town it is imperative that you book a restaurant well in advance. This gives your psycho the opportunity to obsess and muse on your motives, and fully exploit this in the public domain of the restaurant. Remember the magic phrase – it' s all your fault.

CASE STUDIES

Dinner date

I have a story about a guy I call 'the pig man.' I met him internet dating about three years ago (he was funny and very intelligent on email) and spent an unforgettable evening with him. He wasn' t psychotic officially but within an hour of meeting him he was regaling me with a story of a lost weekend doing shedloads of cocaine and hiring three prostitutes at once – which seemed an unusual opening gambit. He spent the whole time with me compulsively eating and drinking everything in site, and occasionally trying to kiss me. I stayed out of pure fascination until he freaked out at the waitress for only taking cash at the nice tapas restaurant (where he made me go dutch on all the food he'd eaten), whereupon I finally lost it. His final words were 'I'm not going to see you again, am I?' No.

Spoilt for choice

I met a guy internet dating who was obsessed about cleaning his house. Only he wanted *me* to do it, or he would go into a mood and get quite nasty. He would often ask me to make some toast, nothing out of the ordinary I here you cry, but when I asked if he would like jam or marmite etc, he insisted I should lay out the table with at least fifteen different spreads so he could choose.

Kebab?

I went out with a guy for about two years when I was sixteen who's biggest achievement was that he'd been arrested 56 times before he was sixteen! There are endless psycho tales I could recount about him including him spitting at me and then throwing a plate at me because I confronted him about sleeping with my best friend – which he had!

The best story by far though was one night when we'd been out drinking. We'd both had far too much to drink and went back to his mum's house where he was living at the time. When we got back he started going on about how he wanted a kebab. I kept telling him it was too late and that we should just go to bed and forget about it – and anyway, I knew he had no money. He started getting more and more angry, but, I honestly thought he'd got over it when I finally managed to get him upstairs to the bedroom.

Apparently not. He continued shouting and screaming about how he wanted a kebab until finally he locked the door so I couldn't get out, grabbed my bag and pulled all the money out of my purse. He then proceeded to leap through the closed window of his third floor bedroom. No joke. I was in complete and utter shock. There was glass everywhere and even a comedy, boyfriend-shaped hole in the window! I ran over in time to see him dusting himself off and running off up the street!

At this point, his mum is on the other side of the door wondering what the hell is going on. I was a bit shaken and told her what had happened and she was freaking out but couldn't get in, cos the door was locked from the inside and he had the only key.

About half an hour later he comes back, kebab in hand. His mum completely loses it with him and he's shouting at her until she's had enough and calls the police. He then comes upstairs and starts on me again. I say I've had enough and try to gather up all my stuff. He then grabs my fish tank (which I kept at his) with my two fish – Tom and Jerry – and holds it out the window threatening to drop it if I leave. The shouting continues until he does actually drop my tank, fish and all, out of the window.

I finally manage to get the hell out just as the police are arriving and safe to say I never did go back...

Sweet or salt?

The moment I realised it wasn't going to last with my girlfriend was the day we went to the cinema together. She was already heading for a bad mood when we left – I should've known then.

I bought a mixed box of popcorn (half sweet/half salty). In the middle of the film she asked me to pass her some sweet popcorn.

When I told her that this was impossible as it's all mixed up and looks identical and the only way for me to tell which bits were which flavour would be to eat it, she flew off the handle and started shouting at me calling me a wanker in the middle of the film!

And the best bit was that she knocked the whole box into the air, covering the two friends who were with us and stormed out, shouting, in the middle of this film, that I was being totally fucking selfish, unreasonable and greedy.

Cook book

I once caught an ex boyfriend masturbating over a cookery book. I'm a huge food fan and could almost understand it except that there weren't even any pictures!

Bead sticks

I'm gay and my former partner used to scream uncontrollably, get angry at dust and beat himself over the head with a loaf of french bread. In hindsight it's pretty funny but at the time it was fairly traumatizing.

9

PSYCHO POLITICS

Since the fall of the Berlin wall and decline of communism much of the once repressed world has become liberal and freedom-loving. Ordinary psychos have had to raise their game to even get noticed. Where once a simple outburst at a friends dinner party might have been enough to ruin your life, now it's almost essential to have an awkward tear-filled screaming match on a daytime talk show.

Psychos tend not to follow established party politics. The political psycho is much more likely to be a single-issue loony. Environmentalism is a typical cause.

Thirty years ago it was impossible to imagine that the environmental lobby would have such a powerful hold over the world's governments. Yet world bodies are now openly discussing how best the planet can heal itself after a century of population explosion, deforestation and unprecedented levels of greenhouse gas emissions. Scientists and statisticians have made the whole world sit up and take notice of the impending catastrophe. Would the world have been so accepting of this rational and sane argument had the green psycho not prepared the way by boring us all senseless for decades, banging on about bypasses and badger sets and chaining themselves to every tree that was foolish enough to stand still for 60 years? If the world does survive this seemingly inevitable global disaster it will, of course, be largely thanks to the stirling efforts of psychos.

CASE STUDIES

Kinky veggie

I once spent three months dating a really dedicated vegetarian. Although I indulged in the occasional steak behind her back, I pretty much turned vegetarian to keep her happy, and it was fine; I stopped wearing my favourite leather jacket, and she even persuaded me to wear canvas shoes. It was only when we'd been together for a while that I began to see the other side of her principles. It became clear that she was very kinky, and into S&M. She owned a leather basque, which she liked to wear while using a large leather whip and talking dirty. I quite enjoyed it, but it was always spoiled to for me, because afterwards, without fail, she would burst into tears, saying she felt guilty about the dead animals. It kind of took the fun out of it all.

Right Wing

When I was at university, I managed to pull this really fit, posh girl. Her Dad was an MP somewhere in Surrey, and she was a Young Tory. I don't really care very much about politics, but I pretended to have an interest just to keep seeing her. But when I went round to her flat one day, I was amazed, and a bit scared; my fit girlfriend had got her hair done to look just like Margaret Thatcher, and had bought a navy-blue dress just like Maggie would wear. She'd also got this big, ugly handbag, and really un-sexy shoes. Over the next few weeks, she started doing this really bad Margaret Thatcher voice whenever we were anywhere together. She thought it was funny, but it freaked me out. The final straw for me was when we were in bed, and she called me 'Dennis'. That was that.

Left Wing

I went out with a guy who claimed he was a 'Twenty-First Century anarchist'. What this meant, in practice, was that he didn't have a job, didn't cut his hair, dressed like a Goth, and had lots of tattoos, which I was into at the time. He was quite funny, when he wasn't going on about bringing down the state, and I thought he was weirdly sexy. We'd been seeing one another for a few months, and it was all going well, until I took him home for my Dad's 50th birthday party. When my Dad mentioned that he had been a Civil Servant for almost 30 years, my slightly pissed boyfriend climbed on to a chair in front of my entire family – grandparents, cousins, nephews and nieces – and made a speech in which he called my Dad a 'a slave to the system, and a self-serving, parasitic cunt'. My Uncle, who's normally a very sweet man, punched him in the face, and had to be pulled off him by various other members of the family. Afterwards, my anarchist soon-to-be-ex said he was just joking – but it was a bit late by then.

Motorhead

One evening, when I was in my late twenties, I met and got chatting to this very pretty, Bohemian-looking girl I'd spotted in a bar. At the time, I owned a TVR, which was my pride and joy. I made the mistake of telling the girl this, in the hope of impressing here. Instead of being excited, she was disappointed and angry. She told me that she was an environmentalist, and that, much as she fancied me, she wouldn't dream of being with me unless I sold the car. But I loved that car, and I wasn't sure I would necessarily fall in love with the girl. So I rented a lock-up garage, stowed the car there, and bought myself a bike. In the next two weeks, I was nearly killed more times than I can remember on that thing. But, I did get to go to bed with the girl, and was all great... until the owner of the lock-up phoned to tell me the car was leaking oil. That would have been annoying in itself, but the trouble was, I was out at the time of this call, and the lock-up guy left the message with my girlfriend. When I came home, she had gone – but not before she'd written 'LIAR' in felt tip pen on every item of clothing I owned, and used scissors to cut my duvet up and spell out the words 'PLANET KILLER' on my living room floor.

Preacher man

At about the time of the General Election in 1997, I found myself going out with a fanatical Labour supporter. This guy seemed nice, and normal, but when he got talking about Tony Blair, and the future of the Labour party etc, he was like some sort of Evangelist preacher. It was all a bit worrying, and – as I'm not very interested in any of the political parties – I had pretty much decided to stop seeing him, when he rang one evening, and offered to drop me at the train station the following day, on my way to work. I accepted, thinking that maybe I could use this opportunity to end the relationship nicely, face to face. But, in the morning, when I got in the car, before I even had a chance to drop my bombshell, he drove us straight past the train station and flicked on the car's central locking. He carried on, in silence, for another few miles, and finally parked up in a quiet street in another part of town altogether. He switched off the engine, and then told me that he didn't care if we never had a relationship, but that he wouldn't unlock the doors until I vowed, on my Mother's life, that I would vote Labour. I thought he was joking, but he wasn't. What a nut! We sat in the car for almost two hours, with me trying to reason with him, me trying to get out, and him not letting me. The worst thing about it was that he never raised his voice, or got angry. He just kept calmly banging on. It was totally weird. In the end, he got me to sign a bit of paper saying that I would definitely vote Labour in the coming elections, and then he let me out. I moved back to my parents' house soon after that, in another part of England, and I didn't vote for anyone that year.

Eco Warrior

A friend of mine went out with a guy who was a proper eco warrior type. To the point where they didn't have sex until she went on the pill cos he didn't want to use condoms cos he thought it was too wasteful. He smelt pretty bad cos he didn't wash much – he lived in a treehouse with a bunch of fellow eco warrior types. He would walk down the street picking up any rubbish and putting it in the bin. He refused to ride in cars and would insist on taking the bus places even if one of us was driving and there was room in the car.

All this is fairly admirable (if a little extreme if you ask me) but the weirdest thing was that he had a pet ferret which he kept on a lead and took everywhere with him. My friend only told me after they broke up that he used to let it sleep in the bed (well, his straw mattress-type excuse for a bed) with them! I never did understand what she saw in him...

Hero worship

My ex-girlfriend was obsessed with Alastair Campbell. She used to cut out pictures of him from the papers and add them to the 'shrine' she had above her bed. The final straw was when he resigned and she went into mourning. She would only wear black and insisted on having a minute's silence every day at 11am. The saddest thing was, I think she was more upset by Campbell's resignation than by being dumped by me!

10

PSYCHO SPORTS

The psycho will be a member of at least one gym. And there they are easily identifiable – either using the stairmaster every day for 6-hour stretches or on the rowing machine wearing thick knitted gym gear.

In every survey that I have heard about (from a friend of a friend) the most attractive participation sport for the psycho is, of course, marathon running. The reason for this is at best sketchy but it appears that the pleasure of being able to run alone amongst a large group of people, combined with the inevitable excruciating suffering at the end, all topped off with the chance to wear a deep sea diving suit is too much to resist.

CASE STUDIES

Sporting injuries

I went on a date with a girl I'd met at a party during my early 20s. I was a former national swimming champion and she was a former national judo champion and, for some reason, I was convinced this would mean we would hit it off. I opted to momentarily overlook the fact that she was 5' 2" and I was 6' 4".

The conversation over our first dinner together inevitably turned to our sporting pasts. However, rather than talk of medals and the records, very quickly my date asked me what the worst injury was that I've ever sustained during my years of competitive swimming. Initially I simply assumed she was joking and so moved the conversation on. However, she was insistent and demanded I told her. Reluctantly, I rolled up my left sleeve to reveal a faint, inch long scar that I had received a few years earlier when I had oh-so-heroically cut myself shaving my arms just before a major competition.

I sensed she was not too impressed but without waiting to be asked she seductively pointed to a tiny scar on her neck. 'Do you know what a sacrifice throw is?' she asked. Clearly not wanting to know the answer I shook my head. Slowly and purposefully she described how a sacrifice throw in judo is when you 'sacrifice' all your own weight in order in order to topple you opponent.

In explicit, lurid detail it was explained that the scar on my date's neck was a result of a sacrifice throw that had gone wrong and forced her freshly broken collar bone out through her neck.

Upon conclusion of this little anecdote we sat staring at one another. In silence. For a long time. We never went on a second date.

Compete or Die!

I met my previous girlfriend whilst at my new gym. I had started a New Year's detox and was keen to meet like-minded, healthy people. We saw each other three times a week and enjoyed using the machines and pool together. We began to see each other outside of gym hours and built up a strong relationship. It was only when we became an item that I began to notice some changes in her behavior. She became extremely competitive in the gym, constantly challenging me to race offs and pool lap times. If she won she would tell everyone in sight and call me a weak loser, which would continue at home. It wasn't until I found an itinerary in her gym bag, which had a chart of how many times she had beaten me with a mark out of ten for her performance. It then went on to predict that with the correct training she would be better than me within a few months. I confronted her with this to which she laughed and said 'typical'. I am currently going out with a girl who hates the gym, which is bliss.

11

PSYCHO HEALTH

If you are in a relationship with a psycho you will already have a better than average understanding of medical terminology. During the first few months of your union, you will have learnt all the details of your psycho partner's health history; you will probably be on first name terms with their doctor's receptionist and will be capable of finding the casualty department of your local hospital as if on auto pilot.

You (more than anyone) know that, even though the psycho in a rage is as strong as an ox, in reality they are as weak as a kitten and need to be waited on day and night because they still don't 'feel right in themselves'. Even though they will experience nothing but pain and suffering for the entirety of your relationship I can 100 per cent guarantee that your psycho will outlive you.

NB The average psycho lives for approximately 130 years. They can attribute their longevity to fad diets, ferocious exercise and chain smoking.

The psycho feels pain more deeply and more profoundly than the rest of us. Indeed the average psycho spends more on prescription drugs every year than the whole county of Surrey spends on its fire service.

It would be wrong to categorize your psycho as a hypochondriac. A hypochondriac believes that they are suffering from a condition that already exists and that is recognized by the medical profession. The psycho community has created entirely new conditions tailored to their specific needs. It is crucial that the psycho suffers from a disorder that only they can diagnose. The symptoms sometimes are so subtle and difficult to define that anyone close too the psycho is kept in a state of permanent terror of the subject coming up, lest he or she gets something wrong or somehow, unwittingly, implies that their illness might all be in the mind.

There are certain medical conditions that have been developed specifically for the benefit of the psycho. The one hope for the psycho is that a new branch of medicine has been developed just to treat these conditions.

This new science is referred to as 'Homeopathic Medicine'. This treatment basically amounts to giving the mad person concerned some parsley, nutmeg or nettles and watching in awe as their 'symptoms' clear up long enough for them to get to the shops to blow your savings.

M.E

This is the most celebrated of all the psycho conditions. The symptoms include lolling about, lounging around and speaking very quietly in their 'ickle baby' voice whilst getting you to cut the crusts off their soldiers and pass the remote because they might be just about strong enough to watch Dr Phil.

The good news is that this illness can now be successfully treated by a regular dose of red tablets. If the pharmacy can't find the red ones the patient will have to make do with the blue ones. (M.E sufferers are prescribed so many sugar tablets by their doctors that many have developed severe tooth decay as a side effect).

It is possible that by merely suggesting that M.E might not be a proper disease I will be inundated by letters of complaint from those who have been diagnosed. Of course this won't be for at least another two years.

Irritable Bowel Syndrome

Just as difficult to diagnose. This ticks many of the psycho boxes essential to gaining maximum attention from the caring professions. It's beauty lies in its unpredictability. This is essential if the commited psycho is going to cause maximum disruption at any well planned gathering or event. IBS is in perfect sync with the psycho as the condition is exacerbated by stress. The more stressed the loon, the worse the condition becomes. The worse the condition becomes the higher the levels of stress. This condition provides an invaluable catch-22 to the attention seeking nut.

Anxiety attacks

This is an enjoyable condition for both the psycho in your life and you. Not only do they get to experience your sympathy and understanding, you and the rest of the shoppers in your local mall get to enjoy a little street theatre as your psycho adopts the fetal postion and breathes into a brown paper bag.

Extra points can be scored if you and your nut can get a lift home in an ambulance. (Paramedics are now specifically trained to act as if these attacks are just as dangerous and life threatening as a cardiac arrest).

Bi Polarity

In the non-psycho community this condition is often referred to as 'feeling a bit unhappy' but in the exciting world of the psycho it is a full blown health disorder that can provide the nut in your life with a permanent excuse for ruining another Christmas.

ADHD Attention Deficit Hyperactivity Disorder

This is very interesting for the reason that the sufferer is usually the child of a psycho. Once upon a time in the dark days of medicine, this condition was known as 'Bad Behaviour' or 'mucking about'. The only known cure was a slap or detention. Now in our more enlightened age the child with ADHD is encouraged to self-medicate their illness by biting a teacher or stabbing fellow students.

S.A.D Seasonal Affective Disorder

This is perhaps the cruellest of all the psycho illnesses. The symptoms are almost too painful to report. In short the SAD sufferer feels a bit weepy in November (or July in the southern hemisphere). This debilitating infirmity is usually found in people with really boring jobs. There is no known cure but the sufferer can find some relief by being taken on regular expensive sunny holidays by their ever-understanding muggle.

Migraines

This excruciatingly painful member of the headache family usually strikes just as you and your burden are due to visit your family or go to an important event connected with your chances of promotion. There isn't a chemical on earth powerful enough to even begin to treat this malady. If your loved one is struck down put them straight to bed and sit with them, stroke their hand and watch your life disappear down the drain.

CASE STUDIES

What's Up Doc?

In my early twenties I briefly dated a doctor. I met him on the internet and our first date was basically fine except that he expressed a wish that his patients would 'shut the fuck up' when he was telling them what nasty medical procedure was about to happen to them.

So not Doctor Kildare, but I could live with that.

After dinner, we wandered out of the restaurant and he announced, 'Christ I need a slash' and proceeded to do this against the restaurant wall, right next to the entrance. Being a nicely brought up girl, I decided that this might have been some sort of doctoral bladder aberration and gave him a second chance.

On our second date we had a drink with another doctor mate of his who referred to his girlfriend as 'Shirlie the Girlie' and whom my doctor boyfriend called 'Cunt'. I should have realised at this point that he was not the man for me. The trouble is, my mum brought me up to believe that anything in a white coat is an unimpeachable authority.

We went back to his place – a total pig pit. On his shelf were videos with titles like 'I Spit on Your Grave', 'I Jump Up And Down On Your Rotting Corpse' etc etc. You'd think, as a bloke, that if you were bringing a girl back to your place with a high probability of a shag, you'd hide your esoteric film tastes until you'd got your leg over at least. Not my doctor.

He believed in letting it all hang out. While he went to the toilet I suddenly feared what I was getting into and ran for the door.

He rang me the next day crying and saying he loved me and was only showing his worst side to test me.

Give it up!

I had a girlfriend who gave up smoking but would still buy cigarettes and 'pretend' to smoke them. She would sit and 'smoke' unlit cigarette after unlit cigarette and then just crumple them up and throw them away! We would sit in the pub and people would offer her a light and she'd just say 'no thanks' and carry on. I guess it's better than giving yourself lung cancer but it was a bit embarrassing – and a bit stupid cos she was still wasting loads of money on cigarettes!

12

PSYCHO SEX

Unlike professional boxers the psycho does engage in sex before, after and during a fight. Psychos are obsessed with sex. They talk about it constantly, the subject creeps into every conversation. They eat, sleep and think sex; there is only one problem, they don't really like it so they hardly ever do it.

If you are sharing a sexual relationship with a psycho it is imperative to get an early night. Not so you can get ready for an extended session of bedroom gymnastics, but because the first three hours after getting into bed will be spent comforting the sobbing psycho as they recount, in some detail, their previously sordid sex life. The act may begin with you, but within 30 minutes you will be having a heart to heart about their ex, or their dad, or their dead cousin (usually killed on a family holiday to the Dordogne, in the late '80s)

That of course is now behind them, with you it's different. They want it to be special with you.

You fall for it.

You are now practically celibate.

CASE STUDIES

Short stuff

My ex-boyfriend was obsessed with dwarves, honest to god. Where most boys would be trying to get their girlfriends to watch porn (an idea I certainly wasn't averse to!) he would beg me to put on *Charlie and The Chocolate Factory* and *The Wizard of Oz*. I thought it was harmless and even quite funny until one night in a club he came running over actually dragging a dwarf behind him shouting 'look what I found!' Luckily, the dwarf (who's name was Gary by the way) found the whole thing fairly amusing and we spent the rest of the night dancing with him. It was at this point however that I decided that the obsession had gone a little too far and that maybe it was time to move on.

Naked drinks

From the outset I knew James was a bit quirky, but he was a friend of friend and he seemed nice. I'd met him at a party after a few drinks, and vaguely remembered a few non-sensical conversations, but also a lot of laughter. He called a few days later asking if I'd like to meet up and I figured it was worth a shot. When I arrived to meet him, he was hunched over the bar, nattering away on his mobile phone. He spotted me, said into his phone, 'Okay, speak to you soon grandma', turned to me and declared, 'Just saying hi to my grandma' and gave me a wink. Our evening continued in a whirlwind of disjointed conversation. It was almost like his mind was a spinning merry-go-round as he flitted from one topic to the next without really saying anything. But hey, he was older, had his own business and, as I discovered a little later, had a pretty swish bachelor pad... which is where we ended up after a few too many drinks.

We had a snog on the couch and then quite casually he unzipped his trousers and pulled them down, along with his boxer shorts. Alarm bells went off in my head – but at the same time it was somehow weirdly unthreatening. I called a cab, to give him a clear signal that the evening was going no further, and expected him to put his clothes back on. But no! Instead he decided to take his shirt off too, saying he was hot. So there we sat, on the couch, him naked, me fully clothed, chatting until the cab arrived. He walked me to the door stark naked, and said a polite goodbye. Crazy guy!

GBH

I started seeing this girl during my first year at university. She was in my halls of residence and we hung out with the same crowd, which was really cool. She had told me that she liked to deal out pain during sex, which I thought was pretty cool. This comprised of some biting, scratching and a bit of hair pulling. Although it wasn't really my cup of tea I went with it as she was clearly enjoying herself. After a while she got bored as my tolerance level increased, and she said she wanted to take it out of the bedroom. I thought she meant a bit of kinky stuff outdoors but I was wrong. She started to put deep heat in my pants before lectures so she could see me writhing about around campus. She used to run up to me in the students union and kick me in the balls in front of my mates. The final straw was when she poured Tabasco sauce on my eyelids when I was sleeping and waited for me to wake up. What a bitch.

Fireman Sam

My previous girlfriend was a fucking nut. During sex she had an obsession with Fireman Sam and Trumpton. She would scream out the names of all the firemen from Trumpton and the theme song from Fireman Sam. If she got them wrong I was made to spank her and she would start again. That was just the bedroom. When we were out on the piss she would get so drunk that she would just leave the bar without telling anyone and always get a taxi to her nan's old house. Our relationship only lasted a few months!

Awoke in pain

I like head as much as the next man but one night I was absolutely hammered, which hampered my concentration and then, next thing I know, I wake up and I've been grouted to the bed. Grouted. Stuck down with deep blue grout to my bed! It took hours and lots of body hair to peel the sheets off. Fucking painful.

Cut short...

When I was seventeen, and still a virgin, I started dating this girl. We got pretty intense about one another and quite soon it looked like we were going to have sex. I confessed that I was a virgin and she said that she was too, but that she really wanted to lose her virginity with me, on one condition. I said I loved her, and I would do anything to make her happy. She said she would sleep with me if I had a circumcision. She said she had been told by her older sister that circumcised penises were more hygienic and that both partners would enjoy it more. I wasn't very keen but she said that was the only way that we would get to go to bed together, and it would be well worth it. Then the summer holidays came around, and she went to California to work on a Camp America holiday looking after kids. While she was away, I decided to go through with the operation so that when she came back we could make love.

Over the course of the next six weeks something like three different male doctors and four different nurses all had a look at my cock and all explained to me that I didn't need to have a circumcision. I was adamant; I told them it was something I wanted and that I needed to have it done. So, eventually, they wheeled me into the operating theatre and, when I came round, I had a terrible ache between my legs and a mummified cock swathed in yards and yards of bandage. Never mind, I thought, it'll be worth it. I even said as much to the night porter who explained to me that my stitches had burst, when I was rushed to hospital that evening, my right trouser leg drenched with blood.

A month later when I met my girlfriend at the airport, still a bit sore, but happy, I told her that I'd had the op. She then explained to me that she was no longer my girlfriend, that she had met a guy called 'Darren' doing Camp America, and they had got drunk and fucked one night. I offered to show her my newly streamlined penis, but she politely declined and wished me luck finding love somewhere else.

Doggy style

I dated this gorgeous girl who had a thing about letting her dog watch us while we had sex. It was a little Yorkshire terrier, called 'Snippet', and I hated it. It hated me too, and it certainly didn't like being in the room when we were shagging. It used to bark when we really got going, and would scratch at the bedroom door and whimper to be let out. The girl bought me some ear plugs, and I used those for a bit, but one time the dog got so upset it did a shit on my jeans and I decided enough was enough.

Sugar daddy

I once dated a girl who was a couple of years younger than me who confessed that, ever since her Dad left her family when she was a little girl, she'd always had a thing about older men. I said that it was cool and that I understood. After that the floodgates kind of opened and when we were in bed we'd play these fantasy games where she'd get me to pretend to be older men like Michael Douglas, Anthony Hopkins, even David Attenborough one time. It was a little bit embarrassing but she really got off on it so we carried on. Until this one day; I came home and she started kissing me and we took our clothes off and then from under the bed she pulled out this cardboard mask she'd made. It was of Buster Merryfield, the guy who played Uncle Albert in *Only Fools and Horses*. It had eye-holes and a gap cut for me to put my tongue through. She said she wanted me to wear it while we had sex, and say stuff like 'Lovely jubbly'. I said no and got out of there as fast as I could.

Get ya socks off

I once met a Swiss banker who had stumbled into a gay club. He was pristine and immaculately dressed – the typical disco-bunny clientele. Next thing I know I'm staring at the white ceiling of the gorgeous Merrion hotel in Dublin, musing over the insistent puppy-like yelping he had made throughout sex and wondering why he had point-blank refused to take his socks off. He finally jumped out of bed, threw his clothes on and ran out screeching: 'What would my mother think?!' I never did find out his name...

13

THE PSYCHO AND MONEY

What's yours is theirs, what's theirs is theirs.

CASE STUDIES

Money money money

I dated a guy who was just completely obsessed with money. He earned a shit load and would boast about it to anyone that would listen. He would tell everyone how expensive everything he owned was, yet he would count every single penny. He would insist on going to expensive restaurants that he knew I couldn't really afford and instead of just splitting the bill, would work out exactly who'd eaten what and what they owed – to the point where it was actually embarrassing. If I asked him to buy me some chewing gum while he was at the shop he would ask for the money back. He kept an accounts book of every single thing he spent. He was actually a lovely guy, very sweet and caring, but I just couldn't cope with the whole money thing! About a week after we split up he sent me a text message saying that I still owed him £4.85 and could I send him a cheque!

Rage Against the Machine

I've dated a number of psychos. I dated a guy for a few months who turned into an A1 nightmare after several beers, calling up in the middle of the night claiming to be covered in blood and scared that he'd murdered someone.

I also unfortunately spent several years with a chap who was very taken with purchasing expensive equipment and destroying it when in a mood over something. He threw a Les Paul through the bedroom window, smashed a Hasselblad on the kitchen floor and destroyed our stereo by ripping it off the shelf and pouring coca cola into it in a meticulous fashion. He swung his belt round his head and put the buckle through my car window and claimed it was because he was having a nightmare. And after I asked him to pass me the remote control once, he swung his £1500 Guild guitar around and as I ducked to avoid it, it hit the banister just above my head. That went into the garden in the rain as well, nicely battered. My Dad was gonna come down with his heavies and get him. Oh boy, was he a nutter.

Mean Girl

I went out with the meanest woman in Britain. She looked after every last pound and pence. If I was ever out of cash, and asked to borrow some money, she would note it down in her diary, and make sure to ask for it back – even if it was coins off the top of the dressing-table. If we went out to dinner, we had to go Dutch. Taxis – half each. We owned a house together, and, when we had to pay the joint insurance, she would work out my half exactly. When I look back on it, I don't know how we lasted so long. She was earning a bucket, and was constantly worried about running out of money. Completely nuts.

14

AMERICA'S NEXT TOP PSYCHO

Beautiful people are insane. Be realistic. If you know that you aren't usually attractive to the most gorgeous people out there, and suddenly you become the object of interest of a supermodel I can guarantee that she is a psycho.

The connection between looks and madness is well documented but not yet fully understood. Anthropologists have still successfully to prove the link, but anecdotal evidence suggests that supermodels and rock gods are complete nightmares.

One Norwegian study in 1996 concluded that the reason that good-looking people are more prone to psycho behaviour is because we mortals are prepared to forgive the most insane behaviour if it is displayed by someone hot.

The graph below illustrates the direct correlation between looks and loons:

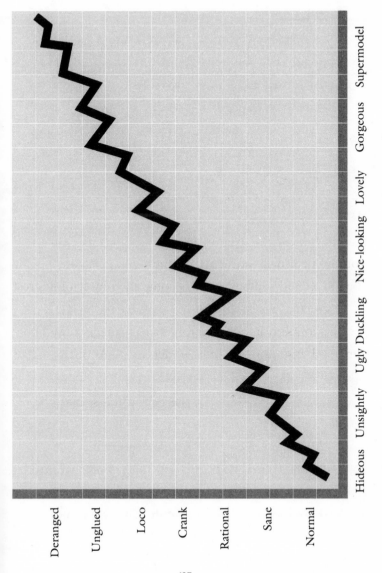

CASE STUDIES

Space Hopper

An old flat mate of mine was stalked by a girl he met in a club. He was very drunk and she pretty much threw herself at him and he ended up bringing her back to ours. To put it politely, she wasn't a small girl, and during the post coital routine interrogation he described sex with her like 'fucking a space-hopper'. From this I deduced that he probably did-n't want to see her again.

A few rejected phone calls later we were in our kitchen on the ground floor at about 2am. My flat mate's room was also on the ground floor at the front of the house, next to the frosted glass front door. I saw a shape moving outside the front door and went to see what it was. I opened the door and there she was, peering into his window! I said 'hi' and she nearly jumped out of her skin! She mumbled something about having the wrong house and scut-tled off into the night.

After that she made regular appearances in the pub where me and my flat mate both worked. Every time she came in he would run into the back and leave me to deal with her and her not-so-subtle enquiries after him. Freak.

Hide and seek

Well I wouldn't know where to start! This guy started dating me knowing I was a model, and slowly
starting to steal my clothes. He blamed my friends,
until it got to the point where I wasn't talking to my
friends any more. Then, a few years later, I found all
my clothes boarded up behind panels in the loft! At
first he denied it but then admitted that he'd done it
so that I never looked good without him!

All Aboard!

I once went out with an super hot Italian guy who
was really fucking weird. He had a fascination with
sellotape and regularly asked me to put strips of it all
over his back, shins, and the back of his hands and
slowly peel them off. He said he liked the way it felt
and used to moan loudly with delight as each bit
came off. It used to take me a good hour to go
through the process, time I would much rather have
spent with friends. But he had much weirder fetishes
in the bedroom. He used to beg me to dress up like

a bus conductor, not in a skimpy ladies outfit, but an authentic vintage 1950s routemaster uniform, because he said it made me look powerful. I didn't oblige, although he always had his Grandad's uniform hanging up neatly pressed in the wardrobe and would gesture to it every time we started to get jiggy. It was a bit of a passion killer to be honest.

Needless to say, the relationship didn't last long.

Never mix work with pleasure

I dated a girl for a couple of years (on and off) who was eight years my junior and a total babe. We met at work, she pulled me at a works drinks. Fantastic fun, great sex but the downside was she had a jealous streak to go with sex appeal. Things that happened over the course were:

Date stamping (she was a receptionist) my expensive white ski jacket 70 odd times with 2 Feb 1999, the date we met. Needless to say the jacket was ruined.

Once, I was popping out for lunch with a couple of work colleagues, she was as nice as pie saying 'Have a nice lunch guys', when I got out the door and put my hands in my coat (another one) they where both full of hand cream!

She once threw a chair at me whilst I was in the bath, and one morning I awoke to find her standing over me with my prized Bill Shankly framed poster. She proceeded to smash it over me, with only my left arm to protect myself! Little did I know at the time that it wasn't framed with glass but Perspex and I got away with just a nasty gash to the arm.

Bottles and knives have been thrown and once whilst I needed to stay at hers for a few days in between flats (she lived with her mum at that time who was equally barking), I returned to hers to find all my gear in a wheely bin. When I turned up, her mum was trying to reverse the car into the drive and I thought I'd give her some direction, only to notice something just about to go under the wheel – it was one of my good shoes! That's when I realised that all my gear was either on the drive or in the bin!

She was even on *Blind Date* when we where going out AND got chosen! She spent a week in Africa with some poor kid from Sunderland, she didn't take any prisoners on that trip. She even ran up a £300 phone bill calling me, which ITV had to pay.

A blinding girl really, but bonkers.

Waterworks

I once went on a date with a psycho girl who I met on the internet. We arranged to meet in a bar and when she walked in I really wished I was Stevie Wonder! It was a really busy bar and we were sharing a table with strangers. An hour in she asked if I'd like to see her again. Foolishly I said, 'I've had a good time, but...' Cue twenty minutes of fairly heavy duty crying. She regained her composure and began to berate me for my choice of footwear, for not being taller, for having a goatee beard (fair enough). We left, she got on a bus and we went our separate ways. Oh, the relief! Until the first phone call. Apparently oblivious to the awfulness of the date she rang at 1am to invite me to a party that she was at, then at 3.30am to her parents'at the weekend and then, at 5.30am, to join her in Camden for a kebab. And again and again.

Photo shoot

I once met a girl on holiday who refused to sleep with me until she'd taken a polaroid of me naked. I agreed, obviously, because I really fancied her. After the picture was taken I asked her what she was planning on doing with it, and she said she was going to add it to her 'collection'. To my horror, she produced a family size photo album from on top of her wardrobe, and proceeded to show me with great delight, countless photos of other naked men. She said she had no intentions of publishing it and that it was just a nice memento. It freaked me out and I left.

Pig masks

I did once have a fling with a girl who, mid-act, suggested we go to the costume shop because 'I really wanna screw you wearing pig masks'.

Picture Perfect

I once 'went out' with a guy who was married. He kept a picture in his wallet that he'd torn out of a newspaper. It was from an obituary of a woman who'd been killed in a riding accident and he said he liked it cos it looked like me. It didn't last long after I found that out.

15

PSYCHO GIFTS

You can be certain that whatever gift you decide to buy, it will not quite be what the psycho in your life wanted. Of course, this will not be made clear to you at the time of opening the present but at 4am when you have:

- No idea what they're screaming about
- No chance to replace said item as the shops are shut

If you have been foolish enough to purchase a psycho a present after a couple of one night stands, you are likely to find that, in the morning, your front room has been smashed up.

CASE STUDIES

Nice presents

When I was living in Brighton my girlfriend at the time got a job placement in Dundee. Neither of us had got much money, and this was before the internet, so we agreed that we would write to one another to try to keep the relationship going. We both wrote loads of letters back and forth but then she started sending me what she called 'keepsakes'. It started with a lock of her hair, and when I said that was sweet, she sent me some nail clippings, then some eyelashes, then some tufts of pubic hair. It was a bit weird and I'd met someone else in Brighton anyway who I was quite keen on, so maybe I deserved the last thing she ever sent me, which was one of her shits, in a tupperware box. Nice.

Ho ho ho

My ex-boyfriend was from Leeds but living in London when I met him. We hadn't been together that long but I knew he had nowhere to go for Christmas so I invited him to join my family for lunch.

Things started to go wrong when he arrived and was flirting really blatantly with my sister! It annoyed me but I was busy helping my mum with the food so just left him to it. It then came to present opening time and he handed me a perfectly wrapped shiny gift. We always take it in turns to open our pressies and after a few rounds of the mandatory socks, scarves and jewelry boxes from the great aunts it was my turn to open the gift from him. I opened it up and inside was the hugest vibrator I have ever seen! I can't tell you how devastated I was! My poor old grandma had no idea what was going on and my mum was just in absolute shock. The boyfriend at this point is crying with laughter – this was obviously his idea of a joke – while I just sat there in silence not really knowing what the hell to do! The boyfriend then starts shouting at me telling me that I have no sense of humour and that I'm an ungrateful little b*tch. He then pushes the tree over and storms out! To this day, my family refuse to talk about what happened (although I now think it's quite funny) and that Christmas is just referred to as 'the one with the incident'.

16

THE SPIRITUAL PSYCHO

All things 'new age' fascinate the psycho. Their unreasonable behaviour and violent mood swings will be nothing to
do with an inability to grow up and become a responsible
member of society. No, the real reason they are in bits, or
silent for days on end, is that their chakras are misaligned
and they have Pisces ascending in their third house.

All psychos have been told that they are a little bit psy-
chic. You will learn this within 20 minutes of your first
meeting. They have been blessed with an insight and sensi-
tivity that eludes us mere mortals. Only seven per cent of
psycho are followers of any religion or belief system – and
even less of a mundane institution like the church of
England. The idea that Jesus is our saviour is way too

prosaic for the hardcore psycho. For their spiritual enlightenment they invariably turn to the east.

Until very recently Buddhism was the faith of choice for the committed psycho. Their entire spiritual being could be expressed by chanting, incense burning and a fundamental lack of understanding of any of the teachings of Buddha. These days the sensitive psycho is more into something called Cosmic Ordering, a creed made famous by Noel Edmonds. Psychos have known all along that the world does not function on a straightforward HARD WORK = SUCCESS + HAPPINESS system. No, they are quite certain that writing down preposterous ambitions on a bit of sacred paper and then secreting this in their sock draw is the only true path to enlightenment.

CASE STUDIES

Religious

At university, I really fancied this very religious girl. She was very sexy but very strict about how she wouldn't have sex before she was married. We started going out and it was all very sweet, lots of hand-holding and kissing, but nothing more. Much as I liked her I was going pretty crazy and she must have sussed this, cos one day she said that we could have 'um sex' because, as far as she was concerned, it 'wasn't real sex'. I couldn't believe my luck. I asked if she was sure and she said yes, totally. She told me that if I wanted to have bum sex I should go into the toilet and take all my clothes off while she did the same, in the dark. I went into the loo and stripped off as quickly as I could. When I opened the door and walked into her pitch-black bedroom, she flicked the lights on and she was standing there fully dressed. Before I could say anything, she threw a book at my cock and sprayed me in the eyes with her deodorant, screaming that I had betrayed her love. Apparently, this was some sort of test and I had failed her, and god too. I've never trusted anyone religious since.

Camelot

I knew a girl who was convinced that she had been a peasant girl in a past life. She made me go to a hypnotherapist and I found myself making up this story about how I remembered being a knight in a past life. My girlfriend was blown away, and in private started calling me things like 'M' Lord', 'My master', and 'My noble squire'. I sort of got off on it though I felt a bit bad about lying. And I felt even worse, when she started bringing home all these books about knights and armour, and kept suggesting we go to castles at the weekends. We got engaged, and at our engagement party, she made this big speech, telling everyone that we were destined to be together, because we'd known each other in the past. Then she read this poem that she'd written me, about how I was her knight in shining armour, and our love had lived on through the centuries, like the legend of Excalibur. I felt awful, but kept quiet, and then one of my mates got pissed and told her that I'd made the whole thing up just to have sex with her. That was the wedding off.

17

THE CYBER PSYCHO

Since the 1990s, with the introduction of the worldwide web, the internet has had an enormous impact on almost every area of human endeavour. Now scientists can share information at the touch of button. Any one of us can view planet earth on our home computers. Doctors in Tokyo can remotely view an operation taking place in Arkansas whilst a business titan in Australia can deal on the New York stock exchange at 3am in his kitchen. More important than any of these seemingly revolutionary leaps in human development, however, is the fact that would-be lovers can now access a psycho at the speed of light without being hampered by any of the obstacles that the real world would normally put in the way.

If you crave the rush of adrenalin that can only come from wondering whether you are going to be made to look an absolute fool by your partner. Perhaps you seek the rush that comes from being driven at a dangerously high speed along a narrow county lane, or from being left naked on your front garden after being thrown out of your own house? Then the world of internet dating is for you. There is no doubt that the mushrooming of internet dating websites has put the psycho within reach of every John and Jane Doe.

Of course there are plenty of people who use internet dating sites who are not psychos. This is a shame, but it need not be the end of the story. With a little determination and some Sherlock Holmes deduction it will be possible to hit the psycho bulls-eye every time, thus enabling you to turn every run-of-the-mill dinner or movie experience into a white knuckle ride where escaping with your life feels like a handsome reward.

Finding your internet psycho

This has been made easier in recent years by the boom in success of the dating website. It seems impossible nowadays to surf the web without some pop-up popping up to help you find true love or chat to literally hundreds of singles in your area. The problem is that most of the users of these sites are sincere, happy and well-rounded individuals, who are using modern technology to widen their circle of friends and perhaps meet that special someone and settle down. They are cluttering up the web and making it more difficult for the rest of us the locate the passive aggressive monster of our dreams.

So: aim high. Simple mathematics tells us that the most attractive and successful people in society are the most in demand; therefore a top model or rock god would only be on a dating website if they had been rejected. If they are cute and single, they are mad. That is why it is crucial only to select the photos of the psycho singletons that are off the scale.

A couple of other things to look out for:

- Their screen name includes the word SEXY.
- In their photo they are resting their chin on their hand.
- Everything else in their photo is in pin sharp focus. They are blurred.
- There are more than 4 photos of them on their profile.
- In their description they include a coded reference to their real email address

- In their description they say that they have been 'hurt many times'
- They are wearing sunglasses on the top of their head.
- They are naked

CASE STUDIES

Disillusioned

I met a guy on the internet who I dated for about four months. In that time he said he wanted to marry me and told everyone, including my mom that we were engaged.

One day I got a phone call from him saying that he was at my house. Seeing as he lived about an hour away, I was quite shocked that he was there. I told him I was at a friend's and he said he would wait. I told him I would be several hours but he still wanted to wait. I told him to go away but I later found out that he went into my house to talk to my mom and tell her about how in love with me he was!

Nightmare. He had to go.

Valley of the Dolls

Cynics of internet dating will feel quite smug hearing about my one and only venture into cyber relation-ships. His picture looked nice, we had similar inter-ests (though in retrospect 'gigs' and 'films' didn't necessarily mean we were a match made in heaven), and I followed all my friends' advice: meet him in a public place during daylight hours, don't wear wear a low-cut top, don't tell him where you live/work/shop etc.

So we met, had a nice enough coffee in Starbucks and he seemed like a pretty down-to-earth guy, bar the slightly greasy hair. Perhaps the caffeine went to my head but when he invited me back to his flat, I accepted, in the face of all the advice I had been given. The house was on a pretty, tree-lined street, inside everything was neatly arranged, but when he showed me into the bedroom my feelings of positiv-ity turned into pure panic.

Arranged neatly on his book shelves, his drawers and lining the edge of his perfectly turned-down bed was the eeriest collection of China dolls I had ever seen, dressed in pristine white dresses, their heads all tilted slightly to the left and bearing sinister little smiles – it was a scene straight from a Stephen King novel. I told him I was going to the loo, made my way out of the front door, ran most of the way home and swiftly removed my profile from the dating website.

Internet date

She seemed perfectly normal and nice, chatting away on messenger so we agreed to meet up after a bit of chit chat. I arrived at the bar and there stood 6ft of lard in black PVC and skull printed clothing, not at all like the picture I'd seen on her profile.

I decided that it wasn't going to be true love, but might be a great friend. This was wishful thinking because as well as being unfathomably ugly, she was a one woman conversation apocalypse, three minutes after meeting me she began a monologue on self harm!

I excused myself with my mobile phone and called my friend from the toilet cubicle. I told her to call the bar and make up some sort of emergency that would involve me having to leave right away. I ran as fast as my legs would carry me round the corner to my life saving friend!

I saw the PVC-clad wide-load months later in

Habitat, where I tried to disguise myself with a set of coasters in front of my face.

Speaka de English?

It was an internet date and my date was a vision of Danish loveliness. On the third date, however, things began to go awry. She told me that she was married but before I had a chance to find out more, three of her Danish friends (male) turned up for some unknown reason. I basically sat there like a tit while they chatted to each other in their mother tongue. Thinking that things might improve I agreed to join them all at a party at a record shop in Soho but, when we arrived, she immediately disappeared, leaving me, once more struggling to find somebody, anybody, who could or would speak to me in English. Two hours later she turned up with a bearded wolfman (her boyfriend I was told) who she had been getting it on with upstairs. I made my excuses...

Soul-less

I met a guy on the internet and we went out on a date. We had a lot to drink (as you tend to do in that situation) and the conversation all got a bit heavy. Among other weird things, he ended up telling me that every time he 'came' he felt like he was losing part of his soul. Needless to say, I politely declined when he asked if I'd like to come back to his...

Racing stripes

I met the Internet loon (although there were no signs at this point) for a date and all was going okay. She was attractive, able to string a sentence together, nice enough if maybe slightly sweaty for the time of year. Anyway, frankly I was just out of a long term relationship and needed a rebound relationship, which ended up being a sort of lesbian Pearl Harbor.

She had a bit of a problem with drink, drugs, bladder control, and behaving normally. I actually felt quite sorry for her and tried to help in some sort of feeble wooly counselor kind of way, but the last straw came with the introduction of poop. During one night of s.e.x I was quite tipsy and it was dark, but became aware that all was not well. I went to the bathroom to find a poo stripe on my nose! I made a quick exit after that.

www.dumped.co.uk

I went out with a guy who I thought was a bit 'jack the lad' and manly but turned out was a blubbering weirdo. After I dumped him, BY EMAIL (you would think that I had made him hate me), he proceeded to hound me with gifts of backstage passes to festivals, CDs, tickets to comedy shows, numerous bunches of flowers and hundreds upon hundreds of soppy emails. As all his emails were sent to my work address – work got so annoyed at my computer always announcing I had new mail that they set my PC up to forward all his emails straight to the bin!

Bullet Proof

I dated this girl once called 'Kat' who I met on an internet dating site (bad start I know). We went out a couple of times for dinner and I took her clubbing in London but she suddenly stopped answering my calls or emails so I left it. I went away to Dublin with work for a week and on my return I opened the mail that had arrived while I was away. Included in my mail was a white envelope. Inside this envelope was another envelope with a cat printed on it. Inside that envelope was something hard wrapped in pink tissue paper. Unwrapping the tissue paper I found a 5.56mm SA80 bullet (I know about these as I was in the TA) with my name engraved on it in capital letters.

J Date

This is a story that happened to me after finding someone on J-Date (for those of you who don't know; J-Date is internet dating for Jews). I'd used it with limited success in the past. This time I really thought I'd got lucky.

This was David's profile: 'Attractive, sensitive with a great sense of humour, is the best way to describe me! I am an active person, particularly in the summer time, and enjoy jogging, tennis, badminton and speed-walking. I own a financial recruitment firm and travel around the world for business and pleasure. I'd prefer my date to be tall, chatty and with a good sense of humour – I love a joke!

References are available upon request :-)'

I contact David, and we decide to go for a Chinese. We have a pleasant evening, and he pays, despite my offers to go Dutch. Soon afterwards, I have to go away on business and, when I get back, I find this email in my inbox: 'Sorry things didn't work out. I suppose you changed your mind. Here is my address for the £30: [Then he supplied his address.] Take care, David'

OK. So David's a bit strange. I didn't respond, and expected him just to leave it. But then he leaves a message on my phone, threatening to sue me if I don't pay my share of the bill!

I don't respond. And, next day at work, before I can even say the word 'psycho', I receive this email: 'Lucy, I wanted to follow up on my email and call to you last night to ensure you received my messages for the £30. Please acknowledge by replying to this email that you will be sending me the £30. I hope you understand from my point of view. Thanks, David.'

Feeling a bit fed up, I write back telling David in no uncertain terms that he has completely pissed me off, and I don't want to hear from him again. I also add that perhaps this is why he has not got a girl-friend.

But did he leave it there? No. HE THEN CUTS AND PASTES HIS CREDIT CARD BILL INTO AN EMAIL!!! And adds: 'Do the right thing Lucy. Thanks, David.'

Four hours later, David strikes again, sending a

text message accusing me of 'Hiding behind email'. He then calls my office and offers up this pearl of wisdom: 'You ate the food, you drank the wine, Pay your bill.'

After another few minutes, he texts AGAIN!! This time, he lets me know that he's called the Golden Dragon restaurant TO REPORT A DISCREPENCY IN THE BILL!

Finally, I receive a call from the Golden Dragon asking me what is going on. When I tell them the story, they not only tell me not to worry about the bill, but offer me a free drink the next time I come by!!

PART 3

18

THE PSYCHO AND THE ARTS

Psycho TV shows

This is a broad church. Not only am I referring to the shows that the psycho might watch, but also to the shows that they are most likely to appear on:

Big Brother
Footballers' Wives
Hollyoaks
Love Island
Celebrity Psychos
Will and Grace
I'm a Celebrity, Get Me Out of Here!

Psycho Books

The Road Less Travelled
Men are from Mars...
The 7 Habits of the highly successful
Who moved My Cheese
Why Men Marry Some Women and Not Others

Psycho Films

Beaches
Fried Green Tomatoes
Field of Dreams
Steel Magnolias
Sophie's Choice
Girl, Interrupted

Poets

Sylvia Plath
Ted Hughes

Psycho Plays

Anything by Harold Pinter
Anything by John Osborne
Anything by Dr Phil

Artists

Van Gogh (anyone who bangs on about how Van Gogh
was a genius who wasn't recognized as such until after
his death is 86 per cent psycho)
Francis Bacon
Lucien Freud
Picasso
Edward Munch

Pop Music

Anything by Tori Amos
Anything by Bjork
Anything by Leonard Cohen

CASE STUDIES

Help!

When I was 17 I lived with a boyfriend who did the following:

- Asked me to walk up and down his naked body in my DMs
- Got me to spit into a little pot which he took to college with him to sip from as and when he felt the need
- Greeted me at the door with a sloppy kiss only to reveal he had red food colouring in his mouth which was now all over half my face
- Regularly bit me hard enough to leave bruises.
- When I broke up with him, he left The Beatles score on the piano that was in the room, open on the song 'The End' (okay, that's just pretentious).

Also, a year or two prior to my going out with him I received in the post a strip of paper about 10cm long and 2cm high with the words 'I Want to Tell You' written on it, and a piece of sellotape wrapped around one end. It only occurred to me after we split up that it must have been from him…!

Psycho after psycho...

Not only have I had one psycho boyfriend, I've had numerous weirdos attracted to me. It seems that in London it's hard to attract normal guys!

I've had a guy who swore blind that he was Jared Padalecki (is that how you spell it? Of 'House of Wax' fame?!) despite the fact that he was called Christian and looked nothing like him! When I confronted him he still swore blind he was the actor and I eventually broke it off. He reckoned I was threatened by his fame. Yeah right.

I broke up with another guy for cheating on me. We were living together at the time so I kicked him out. He then hired someone from Scotland to befriend me, follow me around, and report back to him what I was doing and who I was seeing. He then called months later on my birthday, just to let me know...

One guy had someone kick my door down in the middle of the night when I didn't answer. Apparently he wanted to say, 'Hi'!

Another had his friend call me at 3am so she could scream down the phone that she'd been raped so I'd come out and see him!

And an old favourite of mine – 'You know, you

really remind me of my brother' – during sex.

Stalker

I was a singer in a band back in Perth, Western Australia. I went back to a girl's house (we'll call her Marilyn) after a gig. When she kindly dropped me off home the next day, I casually told her the band would be moving to Melbourne in a couple of months. She pulled over and glared at me. 'But... what about us?' she said, shaking her head. This began two months of utter madness – phone calls, letters, night-time 'vigils' which saw her spending Saturday nights parked outside my house. Watching... Waiting...

Sing-along

Went back to a girl's house, girl's parents house actually; it was about 2am or so. She brought out some wine and some cheese, set the mood with some lights, put on some music (Sinatra, I think) and then proceeded to sing along as though it was some sort of performance that I would enjoy. This went on for about 20 mins or so, and the longer it went on the less I felt I could do to stop it, and the less I understood what was going on.

What really put icing on this cake, though, was the pauses every so often so that she could clear her smokers lungs with violent hacking and coughing. I left when she finally stopped and asked if I wanted to go upstairs.

Self-Portrait

I once went out with a guy who used to make me weird personalised CDs with freaky messages written in what looked like blood (at least I hope it wasn't actually blood!) He'd write me poetry and songs which he would recite/sing to me. Then, when I ended it with him, he drew hundreds of pictures of me and posted them through the door at my mum's house. It sounds harmless but it actually really freaked me out!

Savage Garden

When I used to work at Maccy D's (ashamed now) about four years ago, I dated a girl there called Emma. When I first started she was kinda stalking me and after a week she dragged me outside and said are we gonna go out or what? I said 'err we'll see how it goes first'. She took that as a yes anyway. After two months she wanted to have sex but would only do it with me if I had Savage Garden playing. After about two weeks we broke up as she was irritating the fuck out of me. Also, one night at work she fell down the staffroom stairs and accused me of wetting them to try and kill her. She told everyone this but, unfortunately for her, everyone knew she was a nutter and was lying. I still get mocked for going out with her and my mates call her 'The psycho ex from Maccy D's'.

19

PSYCHO ASTROLOGY

Aries

March 21st to April 19th

The typical Aries is warm and sincere. They are childlike and unpretentious, happy-go-lucky and hard-working.

Aries are born sunny side up. They wake in the morning with a laugh and song. Symbolised by the ram, these tenacious little fellows can move forward through life achieving all their goals whilst still making everyone around them feel good.

Psycho Aries

You will easily spot the Aries psycho: they are usually drunken failures with an enormous chip on their shoulder.

Never visit friends with a psycho Aries. These freaks will find the only stretch of cream carpet and spill red wine on it. And then be sick on it. They like a scene.

Taurus

April 20th to May 20th

Charming, considerate, loyal. Usually good-looking, if not conventionally handsome or beautiful, they will have a way about them that can attract attention. They are very earthy. They are perhaps the most sensual and sexual of all the signs.

Taureans (though very stylish) are not given to being flashy or short-term in its thinking. They know what's important; and you know that there is noone more reliable in whom to place your trust.

Psycho Taurus

Over half of all Taureans are Psycho. To this lot being a psycho is not so much an affliction as an all-consuming hobby.

Everyone enjoys a bit of luxury but these free-loading mind-twisters will fill their wardrobe (with designer clothing) at your expense and then, when you suggest that they might curb their spending, will hit you or sulk, or both.

Taureans can keep a sulk simmering for years, it's only their manic depressive tendencies that can snap them out of it. To give you an idea of how crazy the psycho Taurus is, let me tell you that Adolf Hitler was a regular Taurean.

Gemini

May 21st to June 20th

Fun-loving, witty, attractive. A large number of pop stars, actors, TV presenters and entertainers are born Gemini. If they are not celebrities, they brighten up any group by being the social butterfly of the Zodiac. This sign is young-thinking, bright and alert. They are easily bored, so they are always on the look out for new ventures and adventures.

Psycho Gemini

The symbol for this lot says it all. Where you see the celestial twins, see a split personality. Give these children any responsibility and I guarantee that they will let you down. That may not sound like the end of the world but I mean let you down as in be busy screwing your best friend.

Not a single one of them has any sense of what is right and what is wrong. Allow me to rephrase that: they have only a sense that they are right. Just as you're getting over the fact that they have betrayed and humiliated you, you will get a knock on the front door from a loan company asking you to repay the outstanding credit on the holiday that you knew nothing about but are obliged to fund because you let one of these fantasists borrow your credit card details to pay for some fabricated emergency.

They live on a different planet; you just pay the rent.

Cancer

June 21st July 22nd

Many comedians are cancerian. Not that Cancer is a particularly outgoing sign; just, this lot are a little more sensitive to the workings of human emotions. They are deep and unreadable – the kind of people who can quietly read the world around them and then formulate a point of view that is completely eccentric and unique.

Psycho Cancer

Can you hear that? Can you hear anything above the noise of that sobbing jelly in the corner? That overweight weeping goon has once again managed to show you that their shyness doesn't hold them back from making a complete tit of themselves in public. Of course, you can remember the early days when your Cancerian psycho would stand with you at the edge of a social gathering, making side-splitting comments about the guests at the do, their cruel (but accurate) descriptions sending you into uncontrollable fits of laughter.

But that was a while ago. Now their laser is turned inwards, their poisonous pictures are all self-portraits. If you are with a psycho Cancerian, get out now or your life will become an endless round of watching a comfort-eating whale dripping self pitying tears onto the sixth Hawaiian pizza of the day.

Leo

July 23rd to August 22nd

Brimming over with confidence, the lions will take the lead in any partnership or group. They are almost a little old-fashioned in their belief in honesty, dignity and pride. Best of all, though, those born under this sign are blessed with almost unfair levels of luck. Leos have luck given to them in almost obscene quantities. So they can afford to be generous. They make loyal partners in both romance and business and with their regality they can open doors that are barred to us mere mortals.

Psycho Leo

Get out of the way now because someone is about to throw

a tantrum. That 'adult' with whom you share your life is more than happy to lie on the floor screaming and crying until they get their way.

Don't forget that the Psycho Leo is a hilarious raconteur and can hold the attention of any delighted audience. Of course you won't forget because you will be constantly reminded by the number of faces that look at you with sympathy as your psycho Leo launches in to yet another story about how they 'could have been a professional entertainer'.

Leos will never throw dishes at you, they won't swing a baseball bat at your head, nor will they pull a knife on you, they will, however, treat you like you are dirt under their feet. You will be so drained and demoralised by their self-centred approach that you will fear ever leaving them.

Eventually, however, you will witness a break-through with this selfish tyrant, as they emotionally crumble and beg for your help. Beware! If you have any strength left in you, this is the time to use it for your own escape.

Virgo

August 23rd to September 22nd

Above all, the Virgo is practical. Stereotyped as the guest at the dinner party that wants to do the washing up, the Virgo is the most humble and modest of all the signs. Considering they are so close chronologically to their gregarious Leo neighbours, it is remarkable that Virgos share almost none of their traits. They are prudent, cautious and inconspicuous. Nice people.

Psycho Virgo

Where do we begin?

Psycho Virgos have put seven generations of psychiatrists'children through school. Obsessive Compulsive Disorder doesn't even begin to describe it. The average psycho Virgo considers Howard Hughes to have lived his latter years as something of a filthy slob.

It is not that they are too poor to enjoy themselves, they are simply unable to spend money. All psycho Virgos have savings; almost all of them are millionaires; it's just that they can't dip in to their savings because they are expecting to have to rely on these financial resources some day in the future. That day never has never, and will never, come.

These miserable bastards have one mission whilst they are on earth and that is to make your life a living hell. If you have a single fault they will find it and they will let you know they have found it over and over again.

There are many strange religions and cults around the world practising many weird rituals to discover the paths to enlightenment. But all these rituals will pale into insignificance for any of you unfortunate enough to spend just a week with a psycho Virgo.

You can forget sex as well. To date there is no record of any psycho Virgo being seen naked. These spoilsports are so uptight that they would rather spend the night fitting hypoallergenic mattress covers and vacuum-cleaning pillows than waste their time with something as unhygienic as intercourse with their beloved.

Libra

September 23rd to October 22nd

The only sign of the Zodiac not to be represented by a living thing.

The scales for this sign denote the pursuit of balance.

Their overwhelming need for harmony is the core of their life. It is crucial to them that you are happy, your happiness makes them happy. They like perfection and for things to be 'Just So'.

Psycho Libra

Perverts.

Argument-starting perverts.

There really is no other way to describe them. The

world of pornography is full of Psycho Librans. Of all the psycho signs, this is the one with whom you could have most fun. They aren't violent or controlling, just depraved and always starting rows.

Whilst exhaustively studying the behaviour of the Psycho Libran, I have come to the conclusion that, even though they are distinctly unbalanced, they are actually incredibly good fun. The worst that is going to happen to you is an attack of frostbite from being made to have sex outdoors in winter or someone beating you up when you discover that the carpark your psycho Libran partner has taken you to is not a doggers' haunt after all.

Scorpio

October 23rd to November 21st

Let's face it; even the normal Scorpio is a bit nuts. You don't want to get on the wrong side of the sanest one.

Scorpios are the number one sign to have as a best mate. They will stick with you through thick and thin. They fear no one and will do everything in their power to achieve what they believe is right. They run their lives a little like the Mafia. On the surface they are incredibly friendly and polite, but woe betide anyone who tries to hurt a Scorpio. Scorpions are creatures of passion – they are all or nothing, sensual and serious about everything they do.

Psycho Scorpio

Run away now.

If you know one forget them. They are dead to you now. If you are romantically attached to one, start arranging your funeral because one day they will definitely kill you.

These people are out to take revenge on the world via YOU. They are on a mission to right a terrible wrong that was done to them before time began. They can't really tell you what wrong was done; they only know that they are the victim and they are going to wreak vengeance.

Lots of psycho Scorpios enter the medical profession. Not so much to heal people but to punish disease for having the temerity to exist at all.

Psycho Scorpios have no concept of infidelity. If you are unfaithful to them, you can look forward to a slow and painful death. First, you have to wait until the information has been has been processed, then you will have to sit and watch as the details seep in to their almost purely evil brain, you will witness the rodent-like twitching of their pointy face as they try to grasp the full horror of the crime you have committed against them.

Then you will be killed/paralysed.

I must apologise. I said that they have no concept of infidelity. I should make myself clear. Your infidelity is a corporal offence. Often a capital one. Infidelity on the other hand is their divine right. These people screw around without a shred of guilt. There is nothing wrong in their having sex behind the back of their loyal partner; they are merely expressing the primal instincts that form the sexual DNA of the psycho Scorpio.

You will be cheated on. You will have no right to complain and will be dismembered if you try doing the same thing.

As I said:

Run away now.

Sagittarius

November 22nd to December 20th

The optimists of the Zodiac, Sagittarians can make anything feel possible, a great number of philosophers and visionary politicians are born under this sign.

They are the travellers and adventurers of the Zodiac. They want to go everywhere and experience everything, along the way they want to socialise with everyone.

No matter how low you feel, a Sagittarian will always be able to cheer you up. They are the sign that most believes that everything will be all right in the end.

Sagittarians love words, they love language and expression. They love to debate and argue and enjoy nothing more than having their beliefs challenged on an intellectual level by anyone caring to verbally joust with them.

Psycho Sagittarius

If you have any money saved hide it now.

If it's in the bank, hide the cheque book.

It's up to them if they want to take every illegal narcotic on the planet, it's their business of they want to make a cocktail with a shot from every bottle behind the bar and it's certainly for them to decide if they want to buy yet another bar room full of drunk 'best friends' another round.

These activities are your business because of course you are paying. Yes, the rather mundane part of life, the slightly boring aspect that we all have to face – the PICKING UP THE BILL – is something of a foreign concept to the lovable, huggable psycho Sagi.

After they have gone through your savings to feed their need to appear as a bon viveur to total strangers, they will move on to involving you in committing fraud. Every 'inside job' robbery in banking history has been shown to involve a bank employee worn down by their demanding, whining psycho Sagittiarius partner.

There is hope for you if you are with the Psycho Sag. They will either destroy their veins by searching for another way to get drugs into their sedative-addled body or they will destroy their heart by eating so much fat that it eventually turns in to a buttery lump and stops beating.

Either way you will outlive them.

Capricorn

December 21st to January 19th

Stoic, dependable, authoritative. This most serious of all the signs is the one to rely on if you are in need of a stable, sober guide in life. These people are the realists of the Zodiac. They will err on the side of caution when venturing any opinion. Does this seem rather dull? Not at all, does this precision seem rather reassuring? Definitely.

In this age of soundbites and instant fixes, the glib and the shallow have full rein. We have been slowly swamped by the instant solutions and 30-minute makeovers of the world of pap TV. The Capricorn, though, knows things aren't quite that simple. The Capricorn is right.

Before the Capricorn even opens their mouth to express a point of view, the thought will have been deliberated over for some time and analysed in the adding-machine brain that sits on top of their perfectly postured neck.

We can't rely on very much any more. But we can (thankfully) still rely on a Capricorn

Psycho Capricorn

Booooorrrrriiiiiiinnnnggggg.

These people are so tedious. Every single psycho Capricorn in the world has sailed single-handed around the world. No one cared. No one missed them.

You can look at the rest of the psycho zodiac and perhaps feel a little rush of adrenaline when you think about the danger involved in associating with these freak loners.

Not so with the psycho Capricorn. The only way they will ever try to kill you is by giving you deep vein thrombosis from sitting rooted to the same spot all night wondering how your life ended up in this morgue of a relationship.

The bottom line is that, after five years with this bundle of pessimism, he/she will not attempt to kill you. There will be no need as you will want slit your own wrists.

Ninety per cent of all suicides in the world are committed by the partners of psycho Capricorns. (NB The other ten per cent are by Lithuanians.)

Aquarius

January 20th to February 18th

This is the most altruistic and forward-thinking of all the signs. Aquarians like to explore new ideas and concepts. Often they can explore an idea just for the enjoyment derived from exploring an idea. Aquarians are deeply interested in what the future holds. To that end, they will be the first to own a revolutionary piece of technology – the latest type of television or mobile phone.

The Aquarius is the librarian of the Zodiac. Not that they are quiet and serious, far from it, but they do love to read. They love to fill their heads with new information and to learn new ways of interfacing with the world.

Aquarians are not easily led. They make up their own mind and would hate to be seen as part of the herd. They are individualistic and distinctive.

Psycho Aquarius

Robots, Vulcans and Aquarians. All unable to feel human emotion, these humanoids are the Pinnochios of the Zodiac.

Please don't waste your life with one – they won't notice whether you are laughing, crying or stuck under the front wheel of a VW Beetle.

They like to think of themselves as a new age Leonardo

da Vinci. They are so busy looking at mankind as a concept that they can cheerfully ignore the person right under their nose.

For all their so-called wisdom, they don't seem to realise that everyone thinks they are a bit creepy. If you want a hobby, go out with an Aquarian. Then you can spend the rest of your life explaining to friends and family that 'he/she's not really like that' and 'If you got to know him/her, you'd see what a great laugh they are.'

If you want a passionless and frankly disturbing sex life, I can recommend none more highly than the psycho Aquarian. This androgynous ghoul will take all joy out of the physical side of the relationship and replace it with the romantic equivalent of a watercress sandwich.

They do love a suicide pact, however. So watch out for that.

Pisces

February 19th to March 20th

If Aries is the first and youngest sign, then Pisces as the last is the oldest. The world they inhabit is dreamy and magical. Pisceans are natural artists and even if they don't paint or sculpt they see beauty everywhere.

They are the most sensitive of all the signs. Born under

the sign associated with fish and water, Pisceans can (like water) find their own level in any environment. They are adaptable and fluid.

Pisceans may take a long time to find out exactly what they want to do with their lives, but whatever they decide it will have to be beautiful, and spiritually pleasing.

Psycho Pisces

Fucking weirdos.

Art schools have been churning out these losers for years. These weak-minded pretentious morons have been cluttering up unemployment benefit offices for generations now.

Even if the Psycho Pisces is a heterosexual man his long-suffering partner will still be on the receiving end of the queeniest outbursts, especially if she transgresses some unwritten law like moving one of his hideous ties to the back of the wardrobe.

Somewhere along the line every Piscean will have been told that they are artistic. The psycho Piscean will assume that this gives them license to behave like some kind of super annuated four-year-old, screaming and crying until the are 'heard' and they have their feelings 'acknowledged'.

Many of us go through a stage in our teenage years of thinking that we are sensitive, special and feel things more deeply than anyone else. We get over it. Psycho Pisceans just know they are deeper and feel more than anyone else and for this reason they dedicate their life to attending witchcraft festivals and dying their hair burgundy.

20

EVER DATED A PSYCHO?
(Or are you dating one now...)

Have you ever had to sleep in your car?

A   No

B   Yes, but only because I was trapped in a snow drift.

C   Yes. I daren't go home some nights.

Has any partner of yours ever claimed to be on the run from Interpol?

A   No

B   Yes. It all turned out to be a mistake. We laugh about it now.

C   Don't joke about it. Bunnykins is really scared of being tracked down. I think it's the worry that drives us both to drink.

Have you ever had a knife pulled on you?

A No

B Funny you should ask that, once in Florida we were nearly mugged in the street. Luckily, a patrol car was passing so the mugger ran away. We certainly didn't let it ruin the holiday.

C Yes. But I suppose I was asking for it. I really did have the TV on too loud.

Have you ever come home to find your walls daubed in vicious expletives written in blood or lipstick?

A No

B When we came back from honeymoon, the guys from the rugby club had covered everything in our bedroom with paint and whipped cream. They really are buggers. It was hilarious.

C Yes. It's like something takes her over. Her expression goes blank and I know it's time to get out of the way. She really does regret it in the morning. Usually we do the clearing up together.

What is a restraining order?

A I don't know

B Is it a new religious movement?

C It is an order made upon application of one party forbidding the other party to do something. *Temporary Restraining Order* – Restraining order while case is pending. *Permanent Restraining Order* – Restraining order made in final judgment.

Did you meet on the web?

A No, at a friend's party.

B In a way, yes. It was through logging on to Friends Reunited. We rekindled a school romance. A really lovely surprise.

C Yes. I've had to change my email address and get a new phone. The police think if the letters keeping arriving that I should think about moving home.

Did you get married in red?

A No – a beautiful cream silk dress!

B Yes, we dressed up as tomatoes for comic relief. We raised £1500.

C We chose red as the colour of passion – we are very passionate people.

Have you ever had to apologise to the neighbours about the noise?

A Certainly not!

B Well, there was this time when we had just got back from holiday and the chap from Number 8 told us that our burglar alarm had been going on and off all week. It was quite embarrassing.

C Yes, but Lucy needs to express herself vocally when we are making love – she's a very creative person.

At home, do you talk in a quiet whisper so as not to disturb your loved one?

A Why would I do that?

B Yes, but he works shifts, and he's a light sleeper.

C Of course. She gets terrible migraines. I've seen first-hand how she suffers. She's not putting it on.

Do you know what time Dr Phil is on?

A Who?

B Yes, but only because my favourite show comes on just after it finishes.

C No need, it is automatically recorded on Sky+. And anyway we have the DVD box set.

Have you had your tyres slashed?

A No

B Yes. I think it was local kids. It was just the once but very annoying all the same.

C We were having a trial separation. My car means a lot to me. I think it was an act of love.

Do you have a lock on the medicine cabinet?

A No

B Yes, with youngsters in the house it's better to be on the safe side. Kids can be so curious.

C Yes. Since the 'incident', I think it's better to remove temptation. It's not that I don't trust my special sausage, it's just that he can get carried away sometimes.

How many partners have you had?

A Less than 10

B Between 10 and 20

C Between 20 and 100

Who usually ends your relationships?

A Me

B Them

C It's mutual.

You've just split up with a loved one. What do you do?

A Miss them (it could have been so perfect).

B Move on, it was never meant to be.

C Check the underside of my car every morning, looking out for explosive devices.

You have just suggested that your relationship is not working. How does your partner react?

A Takes it on the chin. He could see it coming. Perhaps deep down he knew all along.

B Doesn't give a damn. There are plenty more fish in the sea.

C Picks up a letter opener and lunges at me.

You go away on a company bonding weekend without partners. How does your loved one react:

A Waves me off, and looks forward to a weekend pottering and reading the papers.

B Get a littles annoyed – this was supposed to be the weekend we decorated the spare room together.

C Seems to be hiding in the bushes outside my hotel window.

Your score

Score one point for any As, two for any Bs and three for any Cs

Under 17 points

You have never been near a psycho. You've had so little contact that I'm wondering why you're reading this book at all. If you're reading this in a shop, please just put it back on the shelf, and let the obviously disturbed bloke behind you get a chance to buy it.

18 – 34 points

You've definitely met at least one psycho in your time. Once bitten, twice shy – you tried it, but didn't like it. You like a little excitement from time to time but you don't want to spend your life scared.

35 – 51 points

Congratulations, you have gone for the psycho dating thing in a BIG way. You are a sucker for punishment, perhaps even a psycho yourself! This book can't teach you anything. For you, it's more *This is Your Life* than *Ever Dated a Psycho* – you had all the answers before you even picked it up.